RED RIVER HAUNTINGS

VOLUME FIVE

The Haunted History and
TRUE GHOST STORIES
OF NORTH TEXAS

And Other Strange and Scary Tales

By Natalie Clountz Bauman

© 2020 By Natalie Bauman
All Rights Reserved

Contents:

1. **LAKE TEXOMA AREA AND POTTSORO STORIES**
2. **DENISON STORIES**
3. **SHERMAN STORIES**
4. **NORTH TEXAS STORIES**

Haints, Haunts 'N Hoodoos and the Just Plain Weird Within Drivin' Distance

From Denison to Dallas, Sherman to Dexter, Bonham to Van Alstyne, Whitewright to Jefferson, from Gainesville to Honey Grove and from Grayson County to Ellis County; in this book, you will find more ghosts, haints haunts 'N hoodoos and just plain weird and scary stories from North Texas. In this book, there are many haunted tales from Denison especially, along with the in-depth history behind the story. If you love ghost stories, you will want this book. But even history lovers who are "non-believers" in ghosts will enjoy all the information from the past of our wonderful North Texas! This book is not meant to be a comprehensive listing of these stories by any means, there are many more to be discovered! Also, check out the other Volumes of my Red River Hauntings series of books and enjoy the stories!

NORTH TEXAS STORIES
LAKE TEXOMA AREA
AND POTTSBORO STORIES

Clattering Crockery and Vacuum-Sealed Sheets on Magnolia Street in Pottsboro

This story for me began simply by asking for ghost stories on my Facebook page. Sometimes when you ask, you receive.

Danny Roberts saw this post and related a personal experience of his own in Pottsboro in the not too distant past. He was kind enough not only to share his story but also to share a few pictures of the family home.

"This is my parents' house in the town of Pottsboro on Magnolia Street" from the early days.

This house has been occupied by many people over the decades. In recent history, the Deets and Roberts families have lived here. I have received some information from the Deets family on Facebook and Danny Roberts on my Facebook Messenger: "One night when I was younger, I woke up in the middle of the night and heard the dishes in the kitchen moving and making noise like someone was washing and stacking them. I go in there assuming my mom is up and see what she is up to at this time of night. I go in and there is no one in the kitchen. I immediately get scared and go tell my parents. My mom told me it was just (the former resident), and she's a nice lady. She passed away doing dishes and had a heart attack while doing so."

(Note: I found out who this was and she was indeed a very nice lady who died suddenly at the house while preparing a meal for parts of her family on a Friday night, not washing dishes. She did drop a pan though. But the haunting probably doesn't stem from her. The family who lived there at the time heard noises in the house, especially upstairs, before and after her death.)

I asked him if this dish rattling happened often or just once.

He replied, "The dishes happened every so often, but also, doors would open all the time, by themselves. When I was younger my parents would tell me it's just the house shifting to make me feel better about it, but I knew better because some things just didn't add up growing up in that house."

"I know this is strange, but I remember when I was in 6th grade, I had something wake me up every night anywhere between 3 and 4 in the am. It scared me enough to where I would tell my science and history teacher about it at school the next day."   I asked: Did something touch you in the middle of the night to wake you up? What did you experience when you woke up?

He said: "I woke up one night at about 3:00 in the am, and my door was open for some reason. I was immediately scared and shut it quickly, I tried going back to sleep but was too scared. I put the covers completely over me to block out whatever was scaring me, and I felt my covers vacuum sealing over my body very tightly and when that happened, I ran upstairs and slept with my parents! I was in middle school at the time and told many teachers about it the next day."   I don't know about you, but the covers vacuum-sealing around me by themselves would make a believer out of me that something strange and terrifying was occurring! I would go run to Mommy and Daddy too!

There is more to the story. I asked if anyone else knew about this house on my Pottsboro History Facebook page since the house has been there for as long as Pottsboro has. I heard from several of the Deets and Roberts family. I will summarize what they had to say.

One woman said she and her Dad heard strange sounds before her Mom died. Before they lived there, she was told an older man that was in a wheelchair died in the house.

There was a wheelchair ramp on the front porch. The house then had a screened-in porch and the family had it enclosed, but they would still hear someone come up the old wooden steps, and then they would hear the screen door squeak open when it was no longer there! One day they heard this and her Dad looked out the window, then turned and looked at her to see if she heard it too! Another strange thing that would happen to them in the house – the radio in the kitchen would turn itself on. After her Mom died they didn't notice any more hauntings. She thought her Mom was a little psychic and the spirits liked her. The people who live there now, and for the last 21 years, said their children claim they have seen things but have not experienced anything themselves. I replied to this, that children have been the primary age range who have been experiencing these things.

Below the same house on Magnolia Street in Pottsboro in modern times, still much the same as it has always been through the years.

A NEW UPDATE to the Story at Paradise Cove

"In Loving Memory"-Voices from the Grave

Many of our tombstones have sayings like "Rest in Peace," "Gone, but Not Forgotten," "In Loving Memory." Memories often fail, but it is often said that love lives forever. I have found proof of the resilience of Love.

My part in this story began years ago when I visited the Paradise Cove Cemetery on Lake Texoma and the guide made a chance remark that there was a local legend of a young boy buried there who had been maimed and killed by a local cotton gin boiler explosion over 100 years ago. I felt an instant connection to this boy's story and knew I must uncover the whole story and make sure as many people as possible knew about it. I felt like he wanted his story remembered.   In the early 1940s, many graves had to be moved from their intended peaceful rest to avoid being lost underneath the new Lake Texoma. Of the 2,500 graves moved, there were two seemingly insignificant graves of children moved to the new Paradise Cove cemetery from the old Jones family cemetery north of the Locust area, west of Pottsboro. They only had crudely inscribed field stones for markers. **They could easily have been missed, overlooked. Amazingly, they were not lost, they were moved to a new cemetery.**

However, time was not kind to the Paradise Cove cemetery over the years. It was not maintained, the brush and weeds grew thick and **almost erased the cemetery from**

memory, except for mischievous young people who crept through it at night for whatever nefarious reason. Finally, a few years ago, someone cleared the cemetery. The caretaker at the Paradise Cove resort took me for a tour of the small cemetery and told the poignant story that somewhere a boy was buried here who had been mutilated and killed in a boiler accident about 100 years ago. I looked down at the ground and could feel that someone there wanted to be remembered. As stated above, this haunted me for years until I found a newspaper article from 1899 describing the Henderson & Mangus Cotton Gin's boiler explosion. I thought instantly of that boy. When I have spoken at public meetings about this story, I have encountered people who have also experienced "a presence" at this graveyard, seemingly wanting attention. Someone I know has actually seen the spirit of a boy there.

I did more research. The Henderson Mangus gin was located near Henderson's Ferry near the Red River.

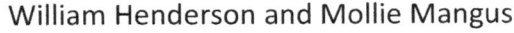

William Henderson and Mollie Mangus

On September 25, 1899, about 1:30 pm, the boiler blew up, completely demolishing the boiler and press rooms. It was reported the blast was so strong, it was heard for miles. Engineer Grant Conder was a young single man who had moved here from Illinois three months earlier. Algernon "Munn" Steele was the new pressman on his FIRST day at work, who had a young wife, Callie and young sons. Conder and Steele were both horribly mutilated and killed instantly.

The boy and girl buried at Paradise Cove are Della A. Jones and Harry W. Jones. They lived in the Brownville, I.T./Locust community and were working near the gin hoeing cotton. They had just stepped up to the door of the lint room building at the gin to get a drink of water when the boiler exploded. They were severely mutilated and were either killed instantly or lived for only a few minutes after the blast. Some newspaper accounts say the boy was named David A. Jones, but further research and testimony from the Jones family has proved that their facts were mixed up and that is the name of the boy's father, David Andrew Jones, a fact backed up by an article in the Denison Sunday Gazetteer, the only paper that got it right.

The boy was named Harry W. Jones, 6 yrs. old, and his sister was Della "D. A." Jones, 15 yrs. old. I have since found members of the Jones family to confirm the names - This information was taken from genealogy notes started by Lizzie Ellen Jones Snow. She wrote:

"Uncle Dave Jones did live in Brownville, I.T, (close to Locust on Red River) and had several children, two of which were, Harry and Della. Harry and Della both died in a gin explosion. After their death, Uncle Dave Jones moved to Arkansas and married an Indian woman. They had two children."

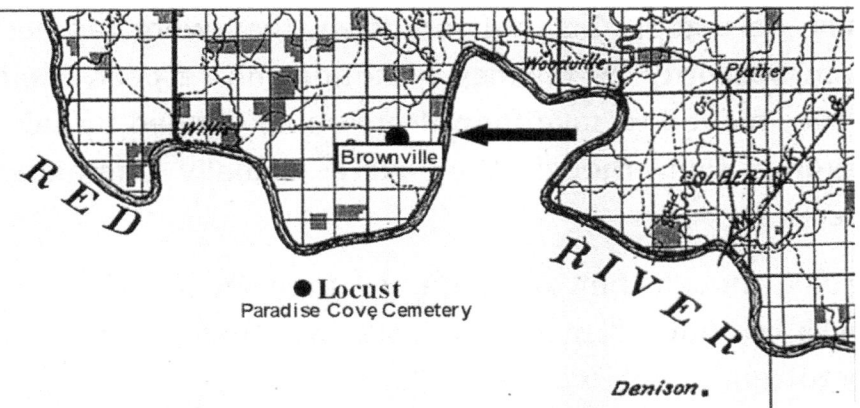

These sources say the boy was decapitated and the girl's legs amputated, from which she died. A member of the family wrote a poem in their honor at the time. This poem/song is listed later.

Another factor that conspired to make sure these children were forgotten is that they were born AFTER 1880 and died BEFORE 1900. They were not recorded in the 1880 census records, the 1890 records where one of them would appear, all burned. They were dead by the 1900 census, so it was as if they never were.

I revisited their graves and found their fieldstone markers, no doubt lovingly etched with crude tools by their parents. The stones were inscribed simply with their initials, the year they died, and one other very important word – "Love."

There have been many factors that may have caused these children to have been erased from history and from memory – forgotten. In 1899, they were lovingly remembered in the best way their parents could. In 1942, they were gone, but not forgotten, they were rescued from obscurity by feelings of honor and respect, their graves moved to save them from being flooded by Lake Texoma even though they were virtually unmarked except for rocks.

Today, though they are gone, yet they speak. The very rocks cry out, "Love" lasts forever. Gone, but never forgotten.

Stone Marker of Harry W. Jones' Grave at Paradise Cove Cemetery Inscribed "1899 H W Jones Love" -- Inscription "1899 D. A. Jones Love" Della A. Jones

Now that their story is known, perhaps Harry and Della Jones can finally rest in peace.

David A. Jones and siblings. Almedia and Savannah Jones standing. L-R: David Andrew Jones (father of the children), William Harvey & James Columbus Jones (X on left knee).

Below is a part of a song written down by an aunt of the Jones children who were killed in the Henderson Mangus gin explosion. Not sure who originally wrote the song.

A song/poem entitled   "The Gin Explosion"

1. Soon as the explosion was over,
   The people gathered around,
   And there the dead and wounded
   Lay prostrate upon the ground.

2. When the sounds had scarcely ended
   The people did bejoin
   To remove them from under timber.
   Soon all four were taken in.

    3. And by aid of kind physicians
       They dressed poor Della's wounds.
       Brownville I.T. has never witnessed
       Such a distress in the afternoon.

    4. Tell me, Father, tell me truly,
       Ere they bear my corpse away,
       Have I been a faithful daughter
       Until this my dying day?

    5. Yes, brave Della, replied her Father,
       Though a faithful daughter you have been,
       And I view the wounds with sorrow,
       Wounds which the explosion made.
       I will see you again.

From Rocky Roberts. This is about the gin explosion of 1899. I sent you a copy of the poem/song that wasn't complete.

Today I found the second half of that poem. Here it is below and has never been published before.

    6. Weep not for me dear sisters
       Shed not a tear for me,
       For I am going to meet Brother Harry,
       Over by the Crystal Sea.

    7. God help the broken-hearted
       That are yet left behind
       To prepare for judgment,
       For tomorrow may be their time.

8. Farewell to my weeping sisters
   Farewell to all around,
   Till we meet on Jordan
   On fair ….. happy land

9. Hark I hear my Savior calling
   Tis His voice I know so well.
   When I'm gone ah don't be weeping
   Sister here's my last farewell.

The last words Della Jones said when she died. Her father composed this song. – from Lizzie E. Snow

But wait, there's even more to the story!

I was recently contacted by David Andrew Jones's Great Granddaughter Retha Lorena Jones, a.k.a. 'Susie', who gave me some more intriguing information about this story, and **yet ANOTHER way these children and their tragedy could have been forgotten.** David was the father of Harry and Della who were killed in the explosion. But the children were not forgotten, even by this segment of the family, because like myself, Retha Jones said she at first didn't know anything about this story or even her great Grandfather David Jones's existence. It was not spoken of in the family. But she felt strongly compelled to uncover her family history which led her to find this story. In her research, she found the story this writer had initially shared about the explosion and the Paradise Cove Cemetery, which caused her to question older family members and family friends further. She found out the children's father, David Andrew Jones, moved east, eventually settling in Arkansas. He married again and had more children, leaving this tragedy, and the graves of his dead children, behind and in the past. **But once again, someone, Retha Jones, saw to it the children were not forgotten.**

One person Retha Jones spoke to in her search was Ed Ponder, a minister. He knew a few stories that were well-known by members of the family and had been passed down through the years. The Jones family has been known to be part Cherokee and have clairvoyant abilities. Della

Jones was 14 or 15 when she was killed in the gin explosion. He said about a year before her death, Della had been out driving cows into the barn. She was then seen to run into the house in shock and fell on the floor. Her mother asked what was wrong. Della said she had just had a vision and it showed her she was soon to die. She was so shocked because she must have seen all the details of the horrible event to come. One year later, the boiler of the cotton gin, on its first day of operation, blew up just as she and her brother walked up to get a drink of water there. On her death bed, Della told them her vision of the previous year had come true just as she had seen.

Tom Jones, another son of David Andrew Jones, the brother of Harry and Della, had a job working at the cotton gin which had been rebuilt. Tom was sleeping about one year after the boiler explosion that had taken the lives of his brother and sister in 1899, and he had a vision in his dream. His dead sister Della came to him and told him "Don't fire the boiler, there's too much mud!" He was sure this was a warning of another imminent disaster, so he warned his boss the next morning about the boiler being in a dangerous condition and urged him not to use it until it was checked. The boss ignored this and proceeded operations anyway. Providentially, Tom was enlisted (or volunteered possibly) to go into town for some supplies and while on his way, he heard a massive explosion just as Della had told him! It is believed another man, perhaps named Atkins, was killed in this explosion. Della's clairvoyance was not able to save her own life, but she was at least able with her warning to save her brother's life!

Perhaps Della was warned of her death to prepare her for it because as her last words in the poem reveal, she spent her last moments comforting those who would be left behind and was ready to pass into the divine and benevolent hands of her Lord!

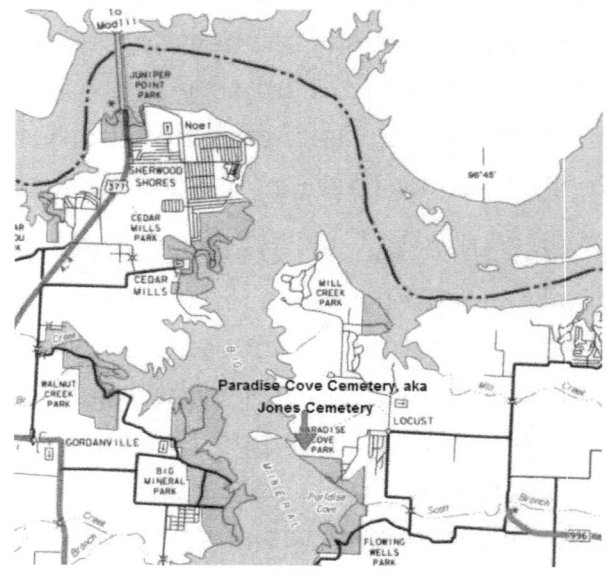

Paradise Cove Cemetery

More About the Haunted Monster Bridge on Squirrel Lane in Pottsboro

A.K.A. Glowing Eyes on the Haunted Creek

Squirrel Lane is located in the Georgetown community off Georgetown Road, northwest of Pottsboro. This is a very short, narrow little country road of little significance. However, it manages to play host to a ghost story or two. There is a small creek, fed by springs near old Fort Johnston, which runs across Squirrel Lane, necessitating a bridge. Old residents will tell you that upon this short bridge, from the dark depths of the creek, can be heard the crying of a young girl. In more recent years, it was the dumping ground of a local murderer who had killed a young woman.

However, now there is more to the story. Several people commented on a post on my Facebook page "Pottsboro Texas History" about this creek and bridge when I asked if anyone had any stories of strange encounters there.

Sherri Morris: I never did, but my grandma Ruth Reeves and my Uncle Danny Reeves used to call it that (Monster Bridge). I am not sure what they saw or heard but they sure believed it was something (strange).

Glenda DeFratus Mahoney: From what I remember Danny's Dad was sitting under that bridge one night after drinking and swore he saw some sort of creature. I stopped on it one time late at night and looked back to see what the sign said that was posted on it and when I did, I saw a hairy large ape-like creature crawling over the top of the rail just above the sign. I screamed (right in my poor cousin's ear) shut my eyes and hit the gas. I never did go back down there. My cousin didn't have time to look back because his ear was ringing, and I was already down the road. He said "what sign" and turned to look at it and that was when I screamed and hit the gas. He didn't see the sign or the creature, but we left there and went to my sister's house. My brother in law tried to get me to go back down there but I wouldn't.

This writer has heard other people who would not be quoted say they know there is a bigfoot-like creature there and others say there are ghosts there as well. I have heard bigfoot/ape-like calls and howls multiple times in that direction myself since I live very close to that location.

Bigfoot at Preston

March 31, 1905 – Some kind of wild varmint caused great excitement in the vicinity of the community of Preston, on Red River, and the country around was afterward being scoured by hunters. C. S. Varney, who lived about two miles southeast of Preston, was aroused on that Wednesday night by a terrible fight between the beast and his dogs. He rushed out with his pistol and saw a very large animal disappear into the darkness and found three of his young dogs had been killed and two of them had been devoured by the beast. Being unable (or unwilling) to follow the beast in the dark, he returned to the house, (great decision). The encounter wasn't over. About daybreak, Varney heard shots at the home of his near neighbor,

W. A. Jackson. Below: Jackson farm at Preston courtesy Grayson County Frontier Village Museum donated by Roy Jackson.

Looking out, he saw a large strange-looking animal headed toward his house. He seized his shotgun and ran out, but the animal fled in another direction. Jackson then came on over to Varney's and a consultation was held. Jackson said he shot at the animal twice and thought he hit it, but the shot was too small to have had much effect on the huge animal. As in the case of Mr. Varney, he was attracted by the barking and yelping of his dogs. Later in the morning, the varmint was seen by a man on the Caddell farm in the bend of the River. Those who saw the strange brute in daylight describe it as being a rather long, big-bodied, dark tan animal with a dark looking back and very large shoulders. Denison Daily Herald. Below: The home of the Caddell family with them in the front at Preston Bend, courtesy of Grayson County Frontier Village Museum.

Bigfoot Today

Bigfoot is still seen, heard, and smelled in the very same area today, over one hundred years later. More about bigfoot especially in Red River Hauntings Volume 2 and wild men in Red River Hauntings Volume 1 and 3.

In very recent times, people continue to report Bigfoot-like creatures make terrifying calls and screams here, preying on pigs that belong to residents there.

The bigfoot seen in this old story was a lighter colored bigfoot. Around the time of 30 years ago, there were also reports of a light colored or white bigfoot around Lake Texoma. It is not known if these normally dark colored bigfoots are albinos or elderly individuals.

In Red River Hauntings Vol. 2, I told about hearing bigfoot howls at night from my yard which came from two points on the south side of Lake Texoma. I recently had this corroborated by someone who was east of the old Preston Bend area and heard these howls as well. They agreed with me that the sheer volume, strength, and duration of the howl was beyond the ability of a coyote. All of us who live in the country know what coyotes sound like and that wasn't it!

There was another bigfoot encounter further to the west on Lake Texoma recently where the informant reported that the bigfoot's joints and bones seemed to crackle when it moved as if it had arthritis associated with old age. But this did not make the creature any less intimidating or terrifying as it charged toward the person in anger!

Bigfoot is sighted VERY often in Hagerman National Wildlife Refuge on Lake Texoma and all along the Red River which is probably a 'highway' for them all through the ArkLaTex, complete with access to vast areas of dense woods for hunting and foraging, rocky ridges, caves and bluffs for shelter and unlimited water supply. These are also very wild remote areas that protect the animals from human interference. Perfect for them.

Bigfoot is commonly sighted all along Lake Texoma and Texas in general both now and in the past:

Wild Man in Fannin County

The name "bigfoot" wasn't invented yet in 1897. Large hairy ape-like creatures were often described variously in terms like "hairy man" and "wild man."

Dallas Morning News June 6, 1897 – This story came from the community of Bailey in Fannin County, Texas near the Red River. In April, a son of W. J. Davis, a renter on the Leonard heirs' land, about one mile south of Bailey, reported a "wild man" had come into the woods where he was chopping wood without giving any warning whatever, and struck him with a piece of timber, then (the wild man) ran hurriedly away from him into the woods. He quit work, went home, and told his parents what had occurred. His parents at first thought he was mistaken or "telling stories," and sent the boy back to chopping wood. When he returned he claimed he saw the "wild man" on two or three occasions, and the tracks were there to show the "wild man" had been where he claimed he had seen him, and he (the boy) was satisfied from the "wild man's" maneuvers he fully intended to do him some bodily injury. He was so completely terrified by the thought, he quit his work and ran home for safety.

The News spread the word that a "wild man" was prowling in the woods south of Bailey, and a crowd of men got together and made a vigorous and thorough search, but could not find him. The result of the search, however, pacified the fears of young Davis and his parents, who firmly believe their boy had seen and been struck by the "wild man." The boy's mother was questioned by the News in the middle of May as to the probability of her son's being mistaken about seeing the wild man and being struck by him, but she gave him to understand she knew her son was not mistaken (or lying) about it.

The wild man was seen again by the Davis family on the night of June 1st in the Davis' yard, by the father this time, and he said the wild man seemed to be very defiant in that he threw rocks and hit his (Davis') house, but finally ran off into the darkness so that he could not be seen. Mr. Davis said he was not aware of having any enemies, at least of the human variety, and could not account for the strange proceedings of the wild man. It was understandable Mr. Davis was very uneasy and afraid this wild man would attack him when he was out at work in the field or the woods and took precautions to take his gun with him everywhere he went just in case.

TARZAN the APEMAN in CLAY COUNTY

Dallas Morning News, Feb 09, 1933 - In Bowie, Texas, interest grew hot and heavy over reports of wild man, who seen scaling cliffs and speeding through underbrush after the fashion of the famous Tarzan. He was believed to inhabit the hilly and wooded section near Newport, Clay County, Texas. Multiple search parties sent out to look for the wild man all reported seeing the bearded hermit. A group from Joy, Clay County headed by P. B. Cox as a guide, went to a cave in which the recluse had previously been seen. When members of the party approached the cave, G. S. Lumpkin and R. D. Allen declared they saw a long-haired and heavily bearded man dash out of one of the three entrances, dexterously scale the cliff above the cave mouth and disappear with startling swiftness into the dense underbrush.

Since then, groups visited the cave almost daily in hopes of sighting the strange and elusive cave-dweller. I'm sure he was smart enough to pick a new cave and the so-called sophisticated people of the town kept coming out to the same old place hoping to see him. He was probably sitting up on the next cliff laughing at them. They deserved it too, you can join in if you like.

Wild Man of the Woods

Dallas Morning News - Jun 12, 1901 - A report had been filed with law officers at Corsicana, Texas that a wild man had been seen two miles northeast of the city in the heavy timber along Post Oak Creek for several days on different occasions. People who saw him said the wild man was very difficult to approach and would run and hide in the timber when anyone came near him.

Great Minds Think Alike

The Norman Transcript.
(Norman, Okla. Terr.),
January 5, 1894

Both Got Fooled.

C. W. Haswell thought he would fool his brother at Pottsborough Texas, by slipping in on him Christmas week. His brother had a similar idea in his head. So it happened that when C. W. arrived at Pottsborough he learned that his brother and wife had taken the train a few hours before his arrival from Norman to visit him. He started back home, and got here just in time to miss his brother. They passed each other at Ardmore.

Feathers Save the Potts in Pottsboro

At Pottsboro, James A. Potts' residence was struck with lightning, completely demolishing one corner of the house. The bolt first struck the chimney, tearing off the whole top, going from there down the gutter to the corner of the house, tearing a hole in the wall, striking the iron bed upon which Mr. Potts and his wife were sleeping, burning a hole in the floor and setting everything on fire where it struck. However, Mr. and Mrs. Potts were sleeping on something impervious to the immense power displayed by the lightning – goose feathers. Down feathers were the gossamer thread which stood between the Potts' and certain death, insulating them from the massive electric shock which otherwise would surely have been their fate. The accompanying rain with the storm soon put the fire out, minimizing further damage to the house.

Coincidentally, at the same time, the Red River was covered with wild ducks – the likes of which had not been seen in years, according to the Sunday Gazetteer, November 17, 1901.

After people heard about the near-tragedy at the Potts and then the saving, insulating qualities of feathers against the lightning, there may have suddenly been a great influx of duck and goose hunters on the Red River to match the overabundance of birds! How ironic that something that just flew in from the sky (bird feathers) could save them from something destructive which also comes from the sky (lightning)! Truly a gift from heaven!

Denison Stories

The Old Oak, a 21 Pound Acorn and a Premonition

Isaac Linley was born in Kentucky in July 1808 and died in Denison, Texas on August 27, 1899. He was an amazing and accomplished man for many reasons. His life was also populated with some rather strange occurrences which will be noted below.

In 1830, he married Louisa Riley, who died in 1858. They had several children. In 1838, Isaac Linley was elected Fulton County, Illinois county commissioner. After this in the 1840s, he served in the Illinois Legislature. In April 1847 he was elected one of four representatives of Fulton County to the Constitutional Convention at Springfield, Illinois. In the early 1850s, he served in the Illinois House of Representatives. He married Mary Josephine Schultz on March 26, 1868, in Rushville, Schuyler, Illinois. They had one child. The Denison Daily News on November 17, 1874, reported Mr. F. R. Brown sold the Farthing property on Gandy Street, consisting of a frame dwelling house and lot, to Mr. Isaac Linley of Rushville, Illinois for $700 cash in anticipation of moving his whole family to Denison in the following spring. Mr. Linley was the uncle of prominent Denison resident, W. B. Munson.

The Old Oak

By 1880, Linley was listed as a widower in Denison on the census. The Denison Daily News on January 22, 1880, gave the sad news that Mrs. Mary Linley, wife of Col. Isaac Linley of Denison, died at his residence of consumption at 3 a.m. Wednesday and was buried at 3 p.m. from the residence. She left a child 12 years old and her husband to mourn her early demise. Her age was 42 years. Col. Linley had been feeble himself for several months and the loss of his companion at such a time must be peculiarly trying.

Isaac Linley at age 72 was once again a widower. Everyone probably assumed he would remain as such for the remainder of his life. But this Old Oak would not be fated to stand alone.

The Texas County Marriage Index has the record of the marriage of Isaac Linley and Josie E. Ivey January 18, 1885. The Sunday Gazetteer on January 25, 1885, also announced the wedding.

LINLEY – IVEY WEDDING

"Wedded love is founded on esteem

Which the fair merits of the mind engage

For these are charms which never can decay."

"Colonel Isaac Linley and Miss Josie Ivey, both of this city, were united in the sacred bonds of matrimony by Rev. Mr. Williams, last Sunday evening at half-past two. The ceremony took place at the residence of Mr. J.T. Ware, 3 miles east of town. Only a few particular friends of the bride and groom were present to witness the interesting ceremony. Several parties from Denison did not arrive in time to see the silken knot tied by the parson, but they got there early enough to congratulate the stately colonel and his blushing bride and do full justice to the refreshments, which included very choice native wines.

Col. Linley is an **old and highly respected citizen of Denison, 78 years of age**, but still vigorous, and giving no indications of being much over 50. He has held many positions of honor and trust in public life, and as a businessman has always been successful and is well supplied with this world's goods. **The bride, who has just entered her 18th year,** has resided in Grayson County several years; for 4 years she attended Prof. Nash's academy in Sherman; and has many warm friends in our neighboring town where she resided so long, who learned to love her for her gentle disposition. Her mother is dead, but her father was present to see his daughter united to the man of her choice. **The Gazetteer congratulates the Colonel upon his good fortune in winning the hand of one so young, so beautiful,** and every way so worthy of his tenderest regard and protection."

The Wise County Messenger on January 24, 1885, put it best: - **"Judge Isaac Linley, seventy-eight years of age was married to Miss Ivey, aged 18, at Denison last Sunday. A line of the poet is thus verified, "The ivy entwines the old oak's boughs."**

The old oak very soon produced an acorn…… a very LARGE acorn.

The 21 Pound Acorn

The Sunday Gazetteer on April 4, 1886, made a startling birth announcement concerning the Linley family. They wrote, "a phenomenal girl weighing twenty-one pounds was born to Judge Linley and wife on Wednesday." This was Julia Fay Linley, born on March 31, 1886. In case you are wondering, as I was, both she AND her mother survived the birth of a twenty-one pound baby! The mother Josie Linley lived until 1957 and her daughter Julia Fay lived until 1952. Amazing! **Then…….. there was ….**

The Premonition

The Sunday Gazetteer reported on August 27, 1899, that all seemed well as Judge Linley woke up, ate his breakfast as usual, except that he remarked at the table he thought he was going to die that day. This was not his usual breakfast table conversation. After the meal, he returned to his bed, fell into a doze, and died at 5 o'clock peacefully without pain. He was 91 years old.

Strangely, people often have presentiments of their impending death. Perhaps people are being prepared for the notion. It didn't seem as though Mr. Linley was very upset by the prospect of dying; he just went to bed for a nap and didn't wake up.

More from the Sunday Gazetteer: "Judge Isaac Linley was a pioneer resident of Denison and was one of the oldest men of Grayson County when he died that Thursday night at his home on West Owings street. For the past 2 years, the deceased has been quite weak from the infirmities of old age. Judge Linley was one of the most aggressive free thinkers that ever lived. He was a great reader and a profound thinker and people were profoundly impressed with his intellectual acumen. He was always ready to defend his convictions and those who crossed swords with the judge usually retired from the contest greatly worsted. He was the most cheerful man that ever lived and his faith in what he believed was right, and never for a moment wavered. He seemed to take a great deal of pleasure in the present life and enjoyed worldly affairs to the fullest extent. The people of Denison were greatly attached to the judge and always gave him a respectful hearing when he was expounding his peculiar views. Very little of the judge has been seen for the past year, but he was always the subject of affectionate inquiry. Of all persons that have passed out of our pioneer life, none deserve a more loving remembrance than Judge Isaac Linley.

W.B. Munson furnished the following brief biographical information: Col. Isaac Linley was born near Mayesville, Kentucky in July 1808. In 1825 he removed to Illinois, where he resided until he came to Denison in 1875. He always took much interest in politics, being a Democrat of the old school, and was well acquainted with Douglas, Lincoln, and other noted men of his time. Before coming to Texas, he had accumulated quite a fortune, which, in the latter years of his life he divided with his children."

The Empty Funeral Procession - If Judge Linley was such a great man and so widely loved and respected, why were there so few at his funeral?

1. "It was a great oversight that no notices were distributed announcing the death of Isaac Linley and the hour of the funeral. He had a great many friends in Denison who would have been present to pay the last respects over his bier had they known of his decease. Owing to this lack of forethought there were very few to accompany the remains to the cemetery - **about a dozen. There should also have been someone to make a few remarks either at the house or the grave.** Col. Linley was a remarkable man who had made history. And aside from this, a residence of a quarter of a century in our midst, demanded that someone pay a becoming tribute to his memory before his remains were placed beneath the sod."

2. "In conversation with Mr. T.V. Munson we learn that it was owing to explicit instructions from Mrs. Welker of Kansas City, daughter of Mr. I. Linley, that no funeral notices were distributed, and no remarks made at the home or at the interment of her father."

3. "We understand Judge Linley's daughter came to Denison about 3 months ago to see her father and she informed the Munson brothers that it was his expressed wish that he should be buried as quietly as possible and that there should be no service of any kind. Of course, this being the case, there were no grounds for criticism, as the wishes of the dead should be respected, however much it may clash with one's opinions of propriety.

The editor of the Gazetteer was an admirer and personal friend of the deceased, and **this paper but gave expression to his feelings when it entered a protest at the seemingly cold and indifferent manner in which the remains of an old and useful citizen were consigned to mother earth**." The Sunday Gazetteer, September 3, 1899.

From the largest baby born in Denison to the smallest babies born:

Denison Daily News, January 26, 1879 - As of this date, Mrs. Lake in Denison was the mother of the smallest baby for its age in the State. It was a healthy girl, three months and three weeks old, and weighed only three pounds. Policeman Wright purchased a handsome doll carriage at Brown's Auction and presented it to the baby. The mother had the baby in the carriage on Main Street the next Saturday.

How small was she at birth if she only weighed three pounds at three months old?

One and One Fourth Pound Baby Born ALIVE in Denison

Probably the smallest child born alive in Denison is at the home of Mr. and Mrs. Sid Allen, on Munson Street. It weighed one and one-fourth pounds in **1902!** This is a truly amazing fact considering this is well before modern technology for the care of very small newborn babies. At the time, this child must have been able to breathe well and in reasonable health. No word on whether or not the child reached adulthood. - Denison Press July 31, 1902

HEALTHY QUADRUPLETS BORN IN 1880 AT CARPENTER'S BLUFF FERRY

A woman of color, living in the Indian Territory near Carpenter's Bluff Ferry, gave birth to four well developed living children Monday morning. The Newspaper was informed by a fisherman living on the Red River who bore witness to the woman who bore healthy quadruplets. (I bet they were small!) This was a VERY unusual occurrence at that time, four babies at once without the aid of fertility drugs or modern medicine, and even more startling, they were all born alive! - Denison Daily News, July 21, 1880.

It's a Grave, It's Gold, No! It's an Empty Hole!!

The Sunday Gazetteer, April 30, 1893 - Sometime during the night on a Monday, part of the kitchen flooring in an old, dilapidated, vacant residence at 1303 West Gandy Street was torn up and a hole was dug underneath. This was discovered the following Tuesday morning by the gentleman residing on the corner east of the house. He noted a general disturbance in the yard which caused him to investigate further. An excavation over four feet long, two feet wide and three feet deep was made under the kitchen.

The hole very much resembled a grave.

This seemed ominous and alarming to the man to have a grave being dug next door to his home, so he sent for the police.

A courier came down Main Street and notified the officers, so Constable J. P. Loving, with several other men, arrived at the scene. Everyone, including the Constable, expected to find a coffin containing the remains of a child or the remains of some unfortunate murder victim. The dirt was removed further down, but nothing was found.

The supposition was then that someone must have dug the hole in search of treasure or buried money. The house was one of the oldest in Denison and the title to the property had been in litigation some years.

Stories had been told of money having been buried there. The occurrence Monday night was probably done by some person who believed the stories and hoped to cash in on them.

The hole was empty Tuesday morning, maybe the treasure hunter found something Monday night after all!

Got Legs? No? Legs Not Required One Particular Week in Denison

The Sunday Gazetteer of Denison, Texas on April 30, 1893, showed it was a week of great variety in Denison on the subject of lower limbs, and one of great inspiration. Just before the weekend, two young men traveling together came to Denison. One of them was without his right arm and leg, the other had lost his left arm and leg. The men went together and would give athletic and acrobatic exhibitions. A hat would be passed around and the nickels, dimes, and quarters seemed to be all in a day's work for them. They found a good way to turn a disability into a decent living. On Monday, a man with no legs was at the Depot. He boarded the train and left for the north at 3:55. Both his legs were cut off between the thigh and knee joints, yet he got around quite well on his own. The conductor and a porter did however have to assist him up the steps on to the train. On Wednesday, a man with deformed legs conducted himself quite well along Main Street in a three-wheeled chair/buggy. On the same day, a man with both legs made of wood from the knees down, came in from the south to Denison to stay for a while. Not only this, but a few blind men were in town selling pencils on the street or doing whatever they could to make a living despite their blindness. It seemed Denison was getting a lesson that week about making the best with what you have, and not letting handicaps hold you back from doing what you want. **As Spock might say ….. "There are always possibilities."**

Man Turns To Stone in Denison

How in the world did a man turn to stone? Ever hear the phrase "scared stiff"? It COULD have happened that way because of an ambiguous article that ran in The Sunday Gazetteer (Denison, Tex.) on February 15, 1902.

It was VERY briefly reported in Denison there was a haunted house in the first ward of the city where a woman killed herself. The article nowhere made clear whether the house was haunted BECAUSE a woman who lived there committed suicide and returned as a ghost; or if a woman who lived in a house which was already haunted killed herself because of the creepy status of the residence in which she found herself. Sometimes brevity in expression fails to express much of anything at all.

Whichever might be the case, however, anyone might be scared stiff there!

But no, that wasn't what happened to this man. It happened on a Sunday. The man wasn't in church when it happened for sure, he must have been otherwise engaged! When seen, he was in the middle of Crawford Street opposite Forest Park.

He was apparently **stone-blind drunk** – paralyzed, helpless and speechless – perhaps even sightless and had to be carried home.

Speaking of people made of stone…..

More About …The Stone / Petrified Woman on the Cursed Corner of 100 W. Main in Denison

The Most Successful Promotion EVER

In several of my previous ghost storybooks, I have mentioned a story about the petrified woman on the Cursed Corner in Denison being found beneath the new Ourand's Saloon building on the 100 block of West Main Street in 1879. In case you thought that story had been thoroughly covered…… well….. it hasn't. Yes, there's more. The Denison Daily News on April 2, 1879, wrote that since the story had been printed in the newspapers, at five hundred people had visited Ourand's Saloon to view the petrified woman. Among the visitors was a well-known physician with a case of surgical instruments under his arm (as if intending to perform a postmortem on the deceased?). The newspaper article did not specifically name the doctor but urged the readers to contact Dr. Nagle for further particulars.

The business manager of the Herald returned from Kentucky and was immediately subpoenaed as a juryman to sit on an inquest concerning the petrified woman with green slippers. The inquest was held at the office of J. D. Ourand, and a verdict of "death by want of circulation" was returned after a few decoctions. (Decoction is a method of extraction by boiling herbal or plant material to dissolve the chemicals of the material, which may include stems, roots, bark, and rhizomes.) Ourand did have a saloon full of "decoctions" of intoxicants after all!

By April 5, the newspaper was printing this: "The petrified woman hoax which appeared in the News on April 1st has been copied extensively by newspapers both north and south the countrywide. All the male knights of the tripod swallowed the story whole, but the astute female editor of the Whitesboro Democrat was not to be duped by such a transparent invention."

One must admit, however, as a promotional device, the story was a roaring success! Mr. Ourand brought in huge crowds to his saloon to see the curiosity, thereby familiarizing themselves with his establishment which was his fondest wish all along! **Bait and switch was born!**

Petrified People Perfectly <u>Possible</u>

Still believe in the petrified woman? It was a powerful story, and it COULD have happened.

This is how her body could have been turned to stone so quickly and this was no hoax:

It happened in Farmersville, Texas in Collin County – The Sunday Gazetteer (Denison, Tex.), March 26, 1899 – "Thursday while W. S. Aston was having his brother Jim's remains exhumed for re-interment in the Odd Fellows' cemetery it was discovered the metallic coffin was very heavy, necessitating about a dozen strong men to bring it to the top. It took six strong men to get the remains in a wagon, and upon unscrewing the lid it was discovered the remains were petrified beyond doubt.

Mr. Aston says he could easily recognize the face of his dead brother. Others of the party say the remains, clothing and shoes were perfectly white and had a polished appearance like plated dinnerware. The fibers of his clothing were plainly visible as were the buttons thereon.

Those who attended the funeral eleven years ago say the day was a rainy one and Dr. A. H. Neathery's theory is that water impregnated with lime ran into the coffin and came in contact with silicic acid forming a silicate of lime."

Any organism can be petrified, turned to stone, and it doesn't have to take a long time. This process occurs when groundwater containing dissolved minerals (most commonly quartz, calcite, pyrite, siderite (iron carbonate), fills pore spaces and cavities of specimens, particularly bone, shell or wood. The pores of the organisms' tissues are filled when these minerals precipitate out of the water, replacing the organic tissue with hard minerals. One of the most common types of permineralization is the silicification mentioned here.

Petrified People Plentiful in Texas

Stone Miners Quickly Turn to Stone

Denison Daily News, September 4, 1877 - An article mined from the Austin Stateman newspaper stated Mr. Lewis H. Shelton, living at Sycamore Spring, on Barton Creek, seven miles from Austin, brought in to the city the petrified breast of a man which he left at Dr. Grant's dental office for an examination. The shape of the chest and ribs was perfect, and there was no doubt the object exhibited was the breast of a man of giant size. Mr. Shelton said he had left the petrified collar bone belonging to the same man and the other half of the breast, at his home, all of which he found on his property. He said twenty miles south of Austin there is in a cave an entire petrified man which was sitting on a stone with a gun across his lap with the was gun also completely petrified.

Considering the one petrified man was holding a gun, he was petrified fairly quickly, proving this could have happened to others as well. He could not have been there more than a few hundred years, and perhaps less than a few decades. Once a miner in Australia found a petrified hat in a mine which he knew to have been there less than fifty years.

He said he wrote to relatives who also know where this cave is located to get more information about it, if possible. Mr. Shelton had visited several mines in that area of Texas which were worked long years before by the Mexicans. Perhaps these petrified men were old Mexican miners or guards who became one of the very rocks which they dug waiting to be "mined" and extracted to the surface themselves.

Since we have seen how quickly petrification can happen (like the guard sleeping on the rock in the mine), if you find yourself in a cave or mine, beware! Don't doze off, keep moving lest you too turn to stone!

Cooke County Catacombs

An amazing discovering was made in a little town south of Gainesville, called Era, Texas. It was named after Era Hargrave, the daughter of an early settler. Judge J. M. Lindsay's donation of six acres for a school in 1878 marked the beginning of the town, although settlers had been in the area since the early 1850s.

Fort Worth Daily Gazette, December 10, 1890 - An ancient sepulcher was discovered by local men Dr. Feares and Major Fidler and by Professor Ashely of Springfield, Ill. It appeared the doctor made his initial discovery six years before this, since which time he spent much of his spare time making investigations. A few months previous, he took Major Fidler into his confidence and the major also became interested in making excavations.

The men would not go into great detail when interviewed, but it was learned the catacomb contained many petrified human remains, very ancient sculptures, and weapons of war. The professor claimed there were clues to dates for these finds that would be of great historical importance. It was rumored that some sort of treasure was found.

The exact location of the cave was not revealed but was supposed to be somewhere on the property of the Hon. Phillip Wethley.

The Fort Worth Gazette, April 16, 1891 - The Clear Creek catacombs were being further investigated by Col. Talby of Dallas. He discovered in another bed the petrified body of a woman along with a very ancient decorative hair comb heavily mounted in gold lying beneath her head.

By 1894, it was thought this same petrified woman and a famous petrified man found in Colorado was being displayed in traveling sideshows all over Texas and the Southwest.

This was often the fate of such finds in those days, sadly, causing them to eventually be lost to future serious study.

Woman Digging for Worms Finds Petrified Man Near Waco

WACO, TX - Fort Worth Gazette, January 12, 1895 — A perfectly formed man, turned to solid stone, one of the best specimens of petrification ever discovered, was found accidentally by Mrs. George Renick, whose husband kept a grocery and saloon (1895's version of one-stop shopping) at the corner of North Sixth Street and Marlboro Avenue in Waco.

Mrs. Renick told the Gazette, "We had set some traps at the river near the foot of Tennessee Avenue. We went down there just after 7 o'clock and while there thought we would fish. My husband and myself were together. In a short time, I took a stick and began digging the earth with it, thinking I might get some worms for bait. In a few minutes, the stick struck something hard. Digging away the dirt I soon discovered a man's foot. It was like stone.

It scared me and I called my husband and we dug the earth away and soon discovered the body of a man. It was lying oriented to the east and west, and the head was about two and one-half feet beneath the surface and lower than the feet. My husband procured a wagon. It took six men to lift the body and in so doing the right arm was broken. We brought it here to our place."

Lying upon two tables was the body, nude and perfectly preserved except for the lower part of the abdomen, where a cavity existed.

A great crowd of curious people surrounded the store and it was necessary to close the business and lock the doors. Several physicians were present and examined the body closely. Dr. H. W. Brown said it was the most perfect specimen of petrifaction he had ever seen. The doctors agreed that the body was that of a white man. They formed the opinion upon an examination of his features and head. Two teeth could be plainly seen, white, and well preserved. The body lay upon the back upon the tables and it could be plainly seen that it was the petrified form of what was once a full-grown and evidently powerful man. It measured slightly over 5 feet 8 inches in length and about 18 inches across the shoulders. Tapping it with a piece of wood or iron produced a sound like that of striking stone. The left arm extended down the side of the body to which it was joined by solid stone. The right hand was placed across the breast, the arm being broken off between the wrist and a point just below the shoulder.

Upon the right hand, what had been a ring in the lines of the skin could be plainly seen. One hair was noticeable in the right eyebrow, and hairs could be seen along the left arm.

Over the heart was a slight depression, which might have been made by a bullet. There were transverse marks just above the depression which might be taken to indicate knife wounds.

Mr. Renick was asked what he proposed to do with his find, and said he had not yet determined. "One man offered me $1,000 this morning for a half interest in it, but I refused."

All morning long throngs were wending their way to Renick's place, bent on seeing the petrified man. Many suspended work to gather about the building and discuss theories concerning the stone man's identity and the number of these grew as the matter was discussed and the day progressed. Work seemed less and less attractive compared to the mystery man.

In the afternoon Mr. Renick had the body moved to a vacant building on the square to be put on exhibition, no doubt craving more space for larger crowds and more money for entry fees.

The prevalent theory for the man's identity was that he resembled a notorious outlaw named Bill Johnson who had committed murder, been hunted down and shot, then hanged in Waco in 1859 on Bridge Street. Old settlers remembered the incident quite well, and Mr. Lewis Powell, who still lived there, was present when the desperado met his death. It appears that after his death, he was buried in the very hollow where the "hard character" was found, which suggests they may have their man correctly identified.

Shortly after the exhibition of the body had opened, it was attached by E. E. Thompson upon a claim against Renick. The latter's wife at once began replevin proceedings, claiming she had found the body and it was HER property.

Several lucrative offers were then made to the Renicks for the purchase of the body. This body was so perfectly preserved, every pore could be seen on the skin and every feature on the face and body was just like that of a living man. Therefore it was considered a very valuable commodity and Renick expected to result in better business to him than selling butter and eggs in the grocery store or German champagne by the glass in his saloon.

The only problem with this unexpected windfall was the proliferation of vultures. Even though this dead body was made of stone, the jackals and other scavengers had gathered to tear off of piece for themselves, or steal the prize entirely for themselves!

In fact, the Honey Grove Signal on January 25, 1895, revealed there was already a lawsuit in the courts for the possession of the body. When you have any valuable commodity, people will usually squabble over possess of it if there is the slightest doubt, even a hunk of rock if people will pay to see it.

Tarrant County's Petrified Man on Little Fossil Creek

Not to be outdone, Tarrant County also now had a petrified man, proclaimed the Honey Grove Signal on April 26, 1895.

The petrification was found by John Hollingsworth near the bank of the Trinity River, five miles below Fort Worth. It was made of limestone and on the little finger of the left hand was found a gold ring. The petrified man was brought to town in a wagon and put on exhibition. (Of course, what else.)

The Post-Mirror. (Pilot Point, Tex.), July 12, 1895 - This petrified man found on April 17th by J. A. Hollingsworth continued to be on exhibit with huge crowds viewing it. It appeared to be a genuine petrification; but since there had been so many fakes circulating, the faith of the public in any petrified man was stretched thin.

This was found 1 ½ miles from Birdville, Tarrant County, near Little Fossil Creek by J. A. Hollingsworth, a responsible and well to do farmer. He first noticed something like a foot protruding from the ground and upon investigation it proved to be a petrified human form.

It was thought to be the petrified body of either Ben Parker, a noted Indian fighter, or Captain Denton, the brave frontiersman after whom Denton County was named, both of whom were killed in 1841 in a fight with the Indians at the mouth of Village Creek. (I don't know why petrified people are usually deemed to be someone famous or infamous, perhaps because they would draw a bigger crowd this way?) It was claimed by some, these people had been buried near where the petrified form was found. (No doubt other people had as well, but of course, there was no way THEY would have become petrified, right?) There was a gold ring on one finger that had the appearance of having been homemade. The relatives of Parker entered suit to have this ring recovered to see if his name was on the inside since they claimed his ring was thus inscribed. No word on the inscription or the result of the lawsuit. (It seems this time, claiming the petrified man was a specific person came back to haunt them!)

Petrified Infamous Outlaw in Gainesville?

The Daily Hesperian, April 6, 1897 - There was yet another petrified man making the rounds, and of course, he was though to be the remains of some infamous desperado. The one in Gainesville at this time had been recognized and identified as a noted bandit from years earlier, although opinions varied as to the exact identity. Some said it was Bill Doolin, or Jesse James, Bill Dalton, Sam Bass or Bill Johnson. (Boy, Bill Johnson really gets around, doesn't he?) The newspaper theorized that soon some other notorious desperado from the past would soon materialize from another block of stone and go on tour with some eager showman selling tickets to provide a cheap, safe introduction to a stone cold killer of the past. Good bet.

Exploding Rocks - Here, There and Anywhere – ANY TIME!

Before entering Earth's atmosphere, larger meteors which caused air bursts or explosions in the air which can cause damage on the ground were usually originally asteroids and comets of a few to tens of meters in diameter, contrasting with the more common and harmless "shooting stars."

The most famous of these was the June 30, 1908, Tunguska, Siberia, Russia destructive air burst which is thought by some to have been either an asteroid or a comet made of iron and ice which entered earth's atmosphere at a very shallow angle and at supersonic speed, causing its explosion.

Eyewitness testimony of Chuchan of the Shanyagir tribe was recorded by I. M. Suslov in 1926 and is as follows: "We had a hut by the river with my brother Chekaren. We were sleeping. Suddenly we both woke up at the same time. Somebody shoved us. We heard whistling and felt strong wind. Chekaren said, 'Can you hear all those birds flying overhead?' We were both in the hut, couldn't see what was going on outside. Suddenly, I got shoved again, this time so hard I fell into the fire. I got scared. Chekaren got scared too. We started crying out for father, mother, brother, but no one answered. There was noise beyond the hut, we could hear trees falling. Chekaren and I got out of our sleeping bags and wanted to run out, but then the thunderstruck. This was the first thunder. The Earth began to move and rock, the wind hit our hut and knocked it over. My body was pushed down by sticks, but my head was in the clear. Then I saw a wonder: trees were falling, the branches were on fire, it became mighty bright, how can I say this, as if there was a second sun, my eyes were hurting, I even closed them. It was like what the Russians call lightning. And immediately there was a loud thunderclap. This was the second thunder. The morning was sunny, there were no clouds, our Sun was shining brightly as usual, and suddenly there came a second one! Chekaren and I had some difficulty getting out from under the remains of our hut. Then we saw that above, but in a different place, there was another flash, and loud thunder came. This was the third thunder strike. Wind came again, knocked us off our feet, struck the fallen trees. We looked at the fallen trees, watched the treetops get snapped off, watched the fires. Suddenly Chekaren yelled "Look up" and pointed with his hand. I looked there and saw another flash, and it made another thunder. But the noise was less than before. This was the fourth strike, like normal thunder.

Now I remember well there was also one more thunder strike, but it was small, and somewhere far away, where the Sun goes to sleep." It devastated a vast area.

This can happen anywhere, anytime. In Denison, on June 9, 1875, the Denison Daily News reported a large meteor passed over the city in a northwesterly direction about a quarter to eleven on that Tuesday night. It became visible about halfway between the horizon and the zenith as a large, brilliant body, moving rapidly, lighting up every object distinctly. After it had passed the zenith, it exploded with a sound resembling that produced by a rocket, shattering into a thousand fragments, which fell in a shower, making a most beautiful display. Just before it exploded, a blue tail was seen to follow it. The course of the meteor was marked for at least a minute after the explosion by a streak of light. The passage of the meteor produced a rushing sound, and immediately after it burst there was a crackling noise, as though the fragments had also exploded. Fortunately for Denison, this explosive meteor did not explode close enough to the ground to inflict damage, but just put on an early fireworks show.

Watch out for the NEXT wandering chunk of rock in the solar system though. We may not be so lucky this time.

Man Cuts Off Finger to Get INTO the Army

Some men might "lose a finger or toe" to keep out of military service; but not so with Major Thomas Thoman of Denison, Texas, the son of a Katy engineer; he voluntarily had one taken off so he could get in. Yes, you heard that correctly! Palestine Daily Herald, March 4, 1918 - Story originally from the DALLAS NEWS, Feb. 25.

Major is not his rank; it was his first name. Major Thomas Thoman walked into the Dallas recruiting station and tried to enlist as a stenographer in WWI, but examination disclosed the little finger on his right hand was crooked and stiff. "That finger will have to come off if we take you," he was told by Sergeant Walsh, probably not believing he would see Thoman again. Without a word, as the Sergeant no doubt expected, Thoman left. But unexpectedly, half an hour later Thoman returned – **with only nine fingers.** "Well, sergeant, I had her cut off," he said. **He was accepted into the army**.

RABIES CREATED LOTS OF GHOSTS

We don't think much about rabies today, except we take our dog and cat to the vet each year (hopefully) to get vaccinated to prevent it. Most don't wonder why. Not so long ago, there was no vaccine for rabies and no cure for it once contracted. Very often, rabid pets bit their owners. There was no treatment available for them except for folk remedies like "mad stones" which when applied to the skin, people hoped would absorb disease from the body. People who contracted rabies would go mad and died a horrible death, so it was feared for good reason.

The Denison Daily News on June 18, 1875, reported G. W. Dismukes of Little Mineral had informed them a little girl there was bitten by what was thought to have been a rabid coon. She was the daughter of Mrs. Denson, residing above the mouth of the Wichita, in the Nation. She was playing just outside the gate, when the crazed raccoon came out from the underbrush and attacked her, biting her on the leg, causing a severe wound. Normally shy, nocturnal animals like raccoons are known to become aggressive in this way when in the advance stages of rabies.

There being no local remedies, the girl was taken to Collin McKinney's home near McKinney, and the mad stone was applied. Collin McKinney's mad stone was known far and wide at the time for its efficacy in absorbing the rabies virus and preventing the disease thereby providing the best chance for life for one bitten by a rabid animal. People would come from all over North Texas to have the famous mad stone applied. (There is more about rabies and the mad stones in my other Red River Hauntings books.) The stone was administered and adhered firmly for thirty-six hours when it fell off and would stick no longer. Mr. McKinney was confident the coon was mad, but was also confident the stone extracted all the virus.

I am not so confident that a conglomeration of stones removed from a deer's stomach and soaked in milk had the power to cure rabies. The next story shows what usually happened to people exposed to rabies who trusted mad stones to cure them. Might as well call a witch doctor.

The Bonham Daily Favorite on Halloween day in 1924 reported a six-year-old boy from Bells who was bitten by a rabid dog died of rabies. A man was also bitten at the same time. He sought modern treatment which was then available for rabies and he was improving. The parents of the child relied on the curative properties of a mad stone and the child died. The Graham Tx Leader and Whitewright Sun newspapers reported on November 13, 1924, that Lark

Wright's shepherd dog bit several children and animals in Savoy, east of Sherman. At first, it was thought the dog was just in a playful mood. Shortly afterward, the dog began to act peculiarly and still a little while later went into fits and died. The dog's head was sent to Austin for an examination of the brain and it was found the animal was indeed suffering from rabies.

The names of the children bitten were Margaret Pierce, Maurene, and Teddy Wright, and Brown Morgan, and they were immediately put under treatment. About this time, it was learned two little boys in Bells had been previously bitten by a large blue dog and one of the boys was showing signs of hydrophobia, from which effects he died Sunday night. The same blue dog was seen several days before in Savoy and had fights with other dogs, and it was believed it bit Mr. Wright's dog. Of the children bitten in Bells by the blue dog, one of them took the new serum treatment the other depended on the mad stone, which did not prove effective against the disease at all.

The rabies outbreak continued west to Denison. The Whitewright Sun on December 11, 1924, had the headline: RABIES CLAIMS LIFE OF DENISON CITIZEN. James Tillman Neil, age 39, died at the City Hospital from illness caused by the October 29th bite from his own dog, which was suffering from rabies. The animal was killed the next day and the head sent to Austin, where examination showed symptoms of rabies. Mr. Neil immediately began taking the Pasteur treatment and continued to do so until just before the writing of the article. Then Mr. Neil was at his job at the Campbell Grocery Company and became ill. He returned to his home and was transferred to the City hospital, where he soon died. **DON'T BE AFRAID OF DOGS THOUGH - NOT ALL NEWS ABOUT DOGS WAS BAD…. (JUST GET THEM VACCINATED).**

Early Prototype for Seeing Eye Dog – Blind Man's Best Friend

We are accustomed to seeing service dogs that help the blind to navigate the world safely. These animals are professionally trained today. But in 1891 this was not so. Dogs to help the blind were not being trained until they were used in Europe in the 1920s to aid blind World War 1 veterans. However, Denison was usually a place where unusual things were invented ahead of their time. The Sunday Gazetteer of Denison, Texas on November 22, 1891, chronicled just such an occurrence.

A blind black man was seen in Denison with a large black dog which seemed very intelligent. When the man got off the train at the depot, he told the dog to lead him to the gentlemen's waiting room. The dog started and when he came to the ladies' waiting room, he first stopped and looked in, then moved off down the platform until he came to the gentlemen's room. Here he stopped, surveyed the premises for a moment, and then conducted his master to an available seat. Later, while leading his master around town, he invariably stopped a moment at every street, crossing to notify his master of the step from the street to the sidewalk, and not only stopped but turned around and watched his master to see that he passed the obstruction safely. The admiring crowd of followers the dog had accumulated was highly impressed with his intelligence and care for his master. **Without meaning to, the talented dog had provided Denisonians with quite an entertaining, unique show not seen anywhere else in the world.**

Another Talented Dog in Denison **BULLY PERFORMANCE**

Nov. 24, 1947 - What "Snoopy," a 5-year-old Boston bulldog can do to a piano solo cannot be duplicated by man or woman, pawing at the keyboard better than most would-be virtuosos, and he vocalizes too. He is a real howling success according to everyone who hears him. This pet of Mrs. Nell Snyder of Denison also plays standing up, as is plain to see. **In a contest between the two dogs in the previous stories, the world's first seeing eye dog without professional training or the singing keyboard wizard of the canine world, which would you choose as Denison's Most Talented Canine?**

SHERMAN STORIES

Phantom Soldiers East of Sherman?

A young farmer by the name of Pate, who lived about four miles east of Sherman, in clearing up some undergrowth in January 1889, found several graves. Instead of giving these graves the respect they should have received, i.e., leaving them to rest in peace, he instead made the unwise decision to dig down into one them until he came to a box, and there he finally stopped. The oldest citizen of that area did not remember any burial taking place at the point where the graves were found. There is a story during the Civil War of an old man, his two sons, and a couple of desperate characters with them, who escaped the conscription officers of the struggling Confederacy, remaining in the bushes and stealing the stock left at home in the possession of the women and the faithful slaves. Their crimes were not confined exclusively to the vicinity of Sherman, but their headquarters were within an hour's ride of the courthouse. One day, a squad of Confederate soldiers captured them in Sherman and started to Bonham with them to turn them into Gen. McCullough. A few miles out, and near where the graves were found by Pate, a party of civilians, old men and small boys, met the soldiers and assisted the prisoners to escape, and the story goes still further to the effect that the civilians were so eager to keep away from the clutches of the soldiers, they strung them up to pecan trees out of reach even of a bayonet. They were cut down the next day and buried in unmarked graves. They were probably the occupants of the graves discovered by Pate. Since these men were killed in such an unjust way, left on cruel display, swinging in the wind in pecan trees for all to see and then their graves disturbed so that even in death they could not rest, would it be strange to think they may still walk the road from Sherman to Bonham? When traveling east from Sherman, watch for phantom soldiers, walking, riding, or even worse, still hanging in a pecan tree. Background of the story from Dallas Morning News, Jan 19, 1889.

Disappearing Drowned Boy – A Ghost?

Have you seen this boy? We hate to get those "Amber Alerts" about missing children. There is a mysterious missing boy in western Sherman who is thought to reside in a pond and only comes out to play with other children. Fort Worth Daily Gazette, July 15, 1887 - In the western part of Sherman, a very mysterious and troubling incident occurred. Two small boys, one about seven and the other about five years of age, were out some distance from a house playing around a pond of water which was about eight feet deep. They ran home suddenly and told their mother another boy who had been playing with them had fallen in the pond and was drowned. Many people and several policemen went to the pond and worked several hours draining the water off through a ditch, reducing its depth to about three feet, and after making a thorough search of the pond, failed to find the body, and abandoned their work without making any discovery. The children both still contended that a boy WAS drowned in the pond and appeared to be greatly troubled about it, but no missing boy was heard of and the mystery remained unsolved.

The other obvious explanation was that the boys did have a phantom playmate that day. He must have been the apparition of a young boy who drowned at some earlier date who decided to come out for a play date.

Who Would Win, Man or Ghost?

On September 7, 1887, people in the black community living on Choctaw Creek south of Sherman said there was a haunted house in their settlement with a family still living there, although it was done greatly to their annoyance and fright. They reported awful sounds emanating from the house at the most uncanny, unsettling, and most inconvenient hours of the night.

It would seem two equally strong-willed entities were at war for possession of that house on Choctaw Creek – the nocturnal, noisy haunting spirit and the brave, persevering family who refused to budge and be driven away.

Unfortunately, the article in the Sherman Daily Register did not record the final outcome of the epic contest, but I would put my money on the brave and intrepid family!

Firemen Think Ghost Sent Off Fire Alarm

Do you think people setting off false alarms today is common? According to the Dallas Morning News on Sep 22, 1936, it was happening then too, with one difference – the alarm was suspected of being set off by a ghost! The Sherman Fire Department was about to hire a ghost detective instead of a Fire Marshal to investigate this problem! Two trucks loaded with firemen and the chief's car had risked lives and equipment speeding to Lamar and Crockett, in answer to an alarm turned in from a firebox on the intersection. The firemen found no blaze and several people standing by declared the box had not been pulled by anyone. Dust on the control lever indicated that human hands had not done the job, but a ghostly mischief-maker.

Further investigation revealed H. D. Griffin, city electrician, was the "ghost."

He had accidentally set off the alarm while working on wires farther up the street (wink, wink).

God Made Me Do It!

Fort Worth Gazette April 11, 1891 – Frank Johnson, an elderly black man, was taken in for insanity. He had been digging for gold in Brook's Grove for a long time, claiming God told him to do so. At least he didn't blame it on the devil, it was the Good Guy this time! (But He doesn't usually tempt people with gold; it could have been 'the other guy' wearing a clever disguise).

World's First Spiderman in Sherman Texas!

This is what people THINK is true - the only Spiderman is a fictional superhero created by writer-editor Stan Lee and writer-artist Steve Ditko. He first appeared in the anthology comic book Amazing Fantasy #15 (August 1962) in the Silver Age of Comic Books. I have ANOTHER truth for you. There was a REAL Spiderman in Sherman, Texas long before this fictional character existed in comic books!

This man could do what a spider can and much more and was recognized as such by his peers in 1919!

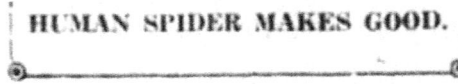

WILLIAM STROTHER
The "Human Spider"

The Sherman Daily Democrat proclaimed on May 28, 1919, William Strother was the "Human Spider." He climbed the Merchants and Planter's Bank building, five stories high, at 200 North Travis Street on the 27th, before a large audience thronging the thoroughfare. He not only scaled the wall of the building (without ropes), he did many other daredevil stunts, thrilling all who saw him, such as climbing the flagpole, standing on his head on the corner of the building and riding a bicycle on the narrow edge of the building always within inches of falling to the street. I bet a spider couldn't do all that!

Green-Eyed Monster Kills a Man in Sherman! Man Was Too Handsome to Survive

Loemy P. Gathright was a successful businessman in Sherman for years. He was the owner of Gathright Bros. Restaurant on Houston Street. However, on June 7, 1915, the Sherman Daily Democrat reported the shocking news he was given a fine of $100 and thirteen months in the federal penitentiary for passing counterfeit $10 gold pieces. Before passing sentence, Judge Russell gave Gathright a chance to make a statement. He said for many years he had led an upright life, but had drifted away from the right way and had recently taken a dark path, but he had made up his mind to tread the straight and narrow from this moment on. He admitted he committed a crime by taking part in the counterfeiting which was discovered by Sheriff Lee Simmons and the federal authorities and deserved his punishment. **Unfortunately for him, this would not be the worst thing to happen in his life. His downward spiral, no matter his good intentions, would continue, and in less than one year.** Apparently, L. P. Gathright was released from prison early, too bad for him. As it turned out, he would have been safer in prison! This page one headline appeared in various newspapers on June 10, 1916 – **Was Too Handsome to Survive - Sherman Businessman Has Eyes Burned Out; Wife Pours Lye on Him.** Dr. H. L. Brown, the physician, was in attendance on L. P. Gathright, and stated he was in critical condition and was rapidly growing weaker, he would lose his eyesight and he had little chance of recovery. His wife poured a quart of hot concentrated lye in both of his eyes at 3:30 a.m. while asleep at his home at 813 West Pecan Street in Sherman and he was seriously burned on other parts of his body. His wife, Mrs. Minnie Gathright, made the following statement to Sheriff Lee Simmons and Deputy Sheriff Arthur Omay, who were among the first on the scene: "I poured hot concentrated lye on my husband. I did not want to kill him, but I wanted to put his eyes out and spoil his handsome face and fix him so he would not be attractive to other women."

Even in the hospital in pain, Gathright pleaded with the Sheriff on behalf of his wife, saying: "I have not done right, and while I do not believe I am as bad as she thinks I am, if I die I hope that she will not be bothered. I hope she will not even be arrested."

He had returned from Fort Leavenworth, Kansas, where he served a short term in the penitentiary for passing counterfeit money. His wife said: "I was mistreated before Mr. Gathright was sent to Fort Leavenworth, and when he returned he told me that he would reform and take care of me and make me happy, and for a while, it seemed he would do it, but other women have come into his life, and I stood it as long as I could."

Mr. and Mrs. Gathright had two grown sons and several smaller children. Gathright was about 45 years of age and was a very handsome man. His face, head, and chest were badly burned by the lye, thus badly affecting his good looks. Very soon, on June 10, 1916, his appearance declined even further when he died. Death soon completely nullified his charming effects on the opposite sex and eradicated his wife's feelings of jealousy. The only people pounding at on their door now were lawmen…. And perhaps reporters.

Mrs. Minnie Gathright was charged with scalding her husband, L. P. Gathright, to death with concentrated lye on June 9, and was **acquitted** in the district court. The Waxahachie Daily Light.

R. L. Polk & Co.'s Sherman City Directory, 1918

Minnie E. Gathright, Widow of Loemy…. Indeed!

Gathright Bros (Carey L and Grayson), restaurant 123 W Houston.
Gathright Carey L (Myrtle) (Gathright Bros), r 417 N Cleveland av.
Gathright Grayson (Gathright Bros), restaurant 214 W Houston, r 425 W Pecan.
Gathright Minnie E (wid Loemy), b 425 W Pecan.

Minnie Gathright lived 21 more years after her husband. She was buried beside her husband in the West Hill Cemetery where they share an elaborate tombstone that says "gone but not forgotten." I wonder if anyone forgot she killed him by burning him with lye? I wonder if he ever haunted her dreams in those 21 years? Or maybe, his handsome face haunted the young ladies who had so admired him before he was killed? After all, it was their illicit attentions which had caused his wife to attack his face with lye in the first place!

Didn't Wait for Lot to Come to Zoar

Here is a story that occurred sometime not specified, and was referred to by the Sherman Daily Democrat in 1920. The situations and names have been changed to protect ….. someone… who knows anymore. A traveling preacher was on his way home one night and he became hopelessly lost. He saw some people and asked where he might find shelter. He was told the only place available was a deserted haunted house down the road. The preacher had his Bible with him, and being therewith armed, he felt safe, so he went there to stay the night. He saw the house had a mailbox faintly inscribed with the name "Zoar." He entered, built a fire in the room, and sat down to read the Good Book. He was reading Genesis 18 about Lot and his uncle Abraham receiving three unusual visitors. Suddenly a small cat rushed past him toward the fire. "Isn't it nice," thought the old man, "there is a cat to keep me company here in this gloomy place?" It seemed the preacher had a visitor himself! Just like Abraham, this visitor was out of the ordinary. Amazingly, the cat arriving at the fireplace ate a live coal of fire and spit out sparks and fire as though fueling up for something…. Something bad.

Alarmed and startled by what the cat did, the old man opened the Bible and began to read aloud for further solace. Before he could go much further, another cat entered the room, a cat about a big as a collie dog. Now he had two visitors! This cat walked over to the fireplace, ate two live coals, and spit out fiery sparks. "When are we going to begin?" said the little cat to the second one. "We can't do anything until Lot comes," replied the bigger cat.

Again, the old preacher sought consolation in the Bible, but a third cat entered the room, interrupting his reading. This one was about as big as a pony, and it ate three live coals and breathed out fire. "When are we going to begin?" said the little cat, and this time the biggest one answered: "You know we can't do anything until Lot comes to Zoar."

All three visitors were here now, it seemed the stage was set for whatever disaster was about to rain down on this location. About this time, the preacher had progressed in his reading of this passage in his Bible to Genesis 19:17 - 26: <u>Flee for your lives! Don't look back! …. But flee quickly, because **I cannot do anything until Lot reaches Zoar.**</u> Then burning sulfur (brimstone) **fell like hail** and **fire rained down** from heaven, destroying entire cities!

The old preacher needed no more prompting and certainly didn't want to <u>**see**</u> who and what would come next. ("Remember Lot's wife," she looked back and turned to salt!) So after this, he jumped up, put his Bible in his back pocket, and raced for the door ready to run for his life. But before he went out, he turned and said to the biggest cat: **"When Lot comes, you can tell him I was here, but I will take a <u>rain check</u> on the fire raining down and keep the brimstone, I'm going to get the hail out of Zoar!"**

(The preacher never knew what happened at the house of Zoar after Lot came since he never looked back. Very wise.)

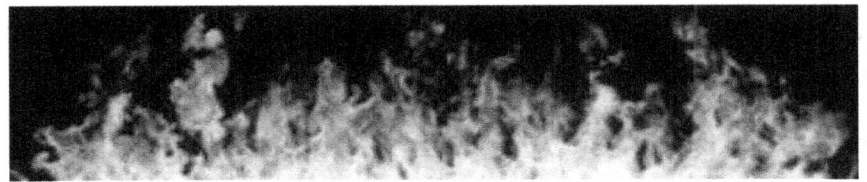

1943 Sherman Directory

WANTED! Dead Animals
HORSES — MULES — CATTLE — HOGS — SHEEP
DEAD OR CRIPPLED—PICKED UP FREE
CALL US COLLECT—DAY or NIGHT
SHERMAN SOAP WORKS, Sherman, Texas   SHERMAN **838**

NORTH TEXAS STORIES

Haints, Haunts 'N Hoodoos Within Drivin' Distance

Copycat Suicide??

If you read Red River Hauntings Volume 3, there is a story about a woman who died in a very unusual way. Mrs. Mary Howser of Van Alstyne was reported missing from the home of her brother Mart Bush. She was not found for a week on August 15, 1898. The dead body of Mrs. Mary Howser, whose disappearance caused great disturbance at Van Alstyne, was found hanging to a fence post in a secluded spot, where the stench attracted the searchers. Her apron had been twisted about her neck and tied to the post not over four feet from the ground. The undisturbed condition of the ground indicated the poor woman sank down and strangled without a struggle. - The Caldwell News-Chronicle August 19, 1898.

This was truly a very unusual method of committing suicide – death by an apron. It wouldn't happen again, right?   Well, it did! Not with an apron, but by imitation.

Imitation Becomes Horrible Reality

Sunday Gazetteer, November 13, 1898 - Leland, the five-year-old son of Mr. and Mrs. Bob Henderson of Van Alstyne, lost his life in an unusual way. He was found by a girl at the end of a rear porch.   When found he had the loose end of a horsetail hair quirt or switch parted, tied, and brought around his throat. The other end of the switch was fastened on a nail. It was less than two feet from the porch floor to the ground, but the unfortunate boy's head was beneath the edge of the porch floor. His feet were touching the ground and his knees were doubled under him. As he could have stood up and the switch would have dangled loosely, it was believed he became frightened and did not know how to take his head from beneath the floor and panicked. In August, a woman was found dead hanging by an apron tied around her neck and fastened to a fence in the nearby suburbs of Van Alstyne.

There must have been much discussion of the tragedy among his family and the story must have made a huge impression on little Leland. His family said of late it had been a favorite pastime of his to take a handkerchief and fasten it around his neck and give his little friends an illustration of how the lady was hanging.

Leland's parents probably thought this was just harmless fun. This last time, his imitation of the hanging was a little TOO good for his own good.

The Gates of Hell in Grayson County

Ghosts and a Geyser Terrorize Whitewright

Whitesboro News, Feb 3, 1888 - Perhaps not since Vesuvius, hurling ashes, fire, rock, and lava over the doomed city of Pompeii, or the earthquake's shock tumbling down massive walls of rock, brick, and iron around the heads of the inhabitants of cities so afflicted, threatening every moment to open a chasm and precipitate them into the seething, fiery gulf below, has the people of a city been so beset, terrified, demoralized and alarmed as the citizens of Whitewright.

A 'yaller' dog was successfully impersonating a meandering cougar just beyond the city limit, and an inhospitable, indefatigable ghost was terrorizing the people within the city. The dog/cougar mutant monster chased the frenzied people into the city and the unfriendly ghost chased them out again and the cycle repeated, ad infinitum.

So between the cougar and the ghost, life ceased to be a blessing for the people of the doomed city.

But wait for it, it gets much, much worse for Whitewright.

Gateway to the bowels of hell in Whitewright:

A traveling man of unquestionable veracity from Whitewright gave the Whitesboro News for its February 17, 1888 issue, the news that Mr. Moorehead in Whitewright discovered a bottomless cave at the bottom of a well he had just dug. Then soon after, a great geyser of boiling water began emitting from the well at intervals of every two hours and twenty minutes. The boiling geyser covered the full diameter of the well's orifice and was hurled skyward to the height of 320 feet and continued to do so for a full twenty-seven minutes! An astounding display, but deadly to be near to be sure.

Not that many Whitewright residents were eager to get close to it, they were far too spooked by now!

Terror of this new wonder in Whitewright prevailed among the awe-stricken people, causing the ghost and the cougar to become objects of only secondary consideration.

An opening to the bowels of hell was believed to have opened within one-half mile of the town of Whitewright. The people were so terrified their end was near, they called for the Salvation Army from Sherman immediately.

Insomnia, the cougar, the ghost, and fears of the emergence of the bowels of hell reigned supreme in Whitewright and its vicinity with property values regularly falling. (Who would want to live there?) It was feared the town itself would be relegated to ghost town status. This fear however, was premature.

At least by 1912, we know Whitewright survived the cougar, the ghost and the bowels of hell and things had improved enough for the city so that they were having celebrations like area-wide picnics. Maybe the cougar died. (I hope it didn't turn into another local ghost for Whitewright's sake!) The bowels of hell probably moved on to a bigger city where there were more people to terrify. The ghost is probably still there, but of the three choices, I think the ghost was the least terrifying and the one least likely to lower property values.

Below: Downtown Whitewright back to normal in 1912 and a cotton yard in Whitewright circa 1900 from SMU Library Collection

City of Dump Has 'Haunted House'

Frank Tolbert called attention to an interesting story in The Dallas Morning News on April 14, 1962. Until I noticed his story I didn't know there once was a city in Texas named Dump in Collin County. You heard it right. Not the city dump, the City of Dump, Texas. Everything IS big in Texas after all and there are a lot of towns and cities. I suppose they finally ran out of names or something to name their town "Dump." More about the name later, it's a bit complicated.

The town of Dump no longer exists except for a few ruins, in memories, in the faded ink of old newspapers and maybe in spirit. But the name wasn't this town's only problem. Dump had a haunted house…..allegedly.

Mesquite resident John F. McCullough's grandfather, Andrew Henry Burns, settled on a farm a few miles north of present-day Wylie in 1848. Mr. Burns opened a general store on the site of Dump, though it wasn't yet called by that name. Before 1899, Dump was called St. Paul because there was a Catholic Church, school, and cemetery by the same name in that community. That year a post office was to be established in a general store owned by Gene Marchant, and they planned to name the post office and the town St. Paul. An official from the postal service came to Mr. Marchant's store saying he couldn't name the town St. Paul because there were already too many post offices in Texas called St. Paul. Mr. Marchant then responded, "I don't care what we call this DUMP as long as we get a post office." The postal official jokingly said, "Why don't you call it Dump then?" Marchant agreed and so it was named Dump, Texas.

Mr. McCullough taught school at Dump in 1899-1900. He would ride a horse out from Wylie daily and single-handedly teach around 85 youngsters "everything from trigonometry to the ABC's." He said a few years before that, a cattle drover died in the combination church and schoolhouse in Dump. This unfortunate fellow took sick during a winter storm, found shelter in the public building, and passed away there. After that, the church-school was believed to be inhabited by a "haint." One morning in 1900, Mr. McCullough arrived for his school teaching chores in Dump to find a crowd of scholars and townspeople gathered around the two-story building. "Listen to the haint in there," he was told. Sure enough, some weird sounds were coming from the first-floor classroom. J. F. McCullough led a posse inside (complete with guns no doubt, once again thinking they could shoot a ghost???) and found the eerie cries of the "haint" were made by a big owl. The bird had come down a chimney into the school heating stove, had become entrapped, and was complaining bitterly.

They didn't find the ghost of the dead cattle drover, but they did set a poor trapped bird free.   OR……….was the owl a manifestation of the ghost?   Native Americans believe evil spirits, ghosts, and witches can appear in the body of an owl. So what exactly WAS released that day?

Voodoo Hoodoo in Paris, Texas

Paris News, Jul 27, 1955 — A strange story of "voodoo medicine" with a tinge of witchcraft came before the grand jury in Lamar County.

First an inquest held in Justice of the Peace W. H. P. Anderson's court brought out details of the eerie incident. A nine-year-old black girl died after apparently being "treated" by a black woman suspected of voodoo practices in Paris, Texas.

Assistant District Attorney C. V. Flanary said the girl had been taken first to a physician in Roxton who advised her mother to take her immediately to the hospital. Instead of doing so, the woman took the sick girl to the suspected voodoo doctor's home in Paris. The girl died later in the night, either en route to the hospital or immediately after arriving there. The DA asserts the girl died from natural causes, and the death was allowed to happen because of the delay in providing real treatment.

The mother testified the witch doctor had treated her once before. "She blew in my eyes and I could see better immediately."

A twin brother of the dead girl was later taken to a Paris hospital because of illness. No word on whether the hospital called in the witch doctor to consult on the case or if anyone blew in the boy's face to make him all better.

Diabolical Ghost Town of Dexter, Texas

Dexter Hip-Deep in Coffins and Ghosts

Dexter was a true wild west town in the 1800s in eastern Cooke County, just west of Gordonville. Check out my book "When the West Was Wild in Delaware Bend" for more history on Dexter and the surrounding area, it is very interesting! The town was named for a famous racehorse and was the scene of many saloons, **murders**, horse, and cattle thefts. This makes the perfect setting for hauntings.

Dexter in 1885

What made the place so creepy is, there was an old vacant drug store labeled "bank" with its early 1900s dust and cobweb encrusted merchandise still on the shelves as if frozen in time, forever stranded in the Twilight Zone of Halloween, complete with advertisements on the walls for Nash's Headache Powders and Dr. Hobson's Toothache Drops. To complete the perfect All Hallow's Eve atmosphere in Dexter was the multitude of old-style coffins lining the streets of the town. It seemed the undertaker had overestimated his clientele and bought WAY too many of those old-fashioned diamond-shaped wooden coffins. In his frustration at the lack of sales, he threw many of them, especially child-sized coffins, all over Dexter. I suppose he was angry more children weren't dying! According to Dallas Morning News columnist Frank X. Tolbert in the 1960s and 70s - even as late and the early 1960s, the ghost town of Dexter (in more than one sense of the word) was covered in coffins, on top of the ground! There were more coffins above ground than buried below! They were up and down the streets and tossed in the weeds in vacant lots.

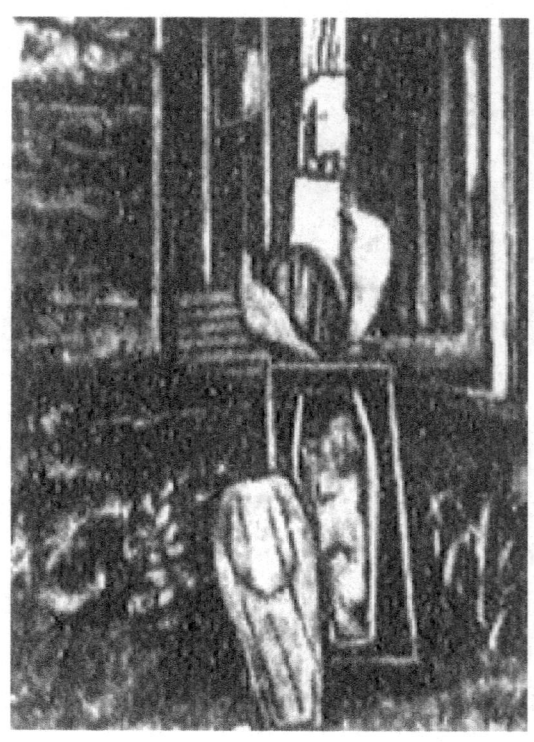

By the early 1970s, someone had removed (or stolen as souvenirs or relics) the old coffins.

By the 1960s, Tol Collum's general store was still open. Mayor W. G. Delashaw had also run a general store here in this building in the 1950s. Even this building was spooky because the red brick building had a skull, yes, a real human skull leering with its empty dead eyes out the second-floor window. Mr. Delashaw said it was used long ago in lodge rituals. Some rumored it was the skull of a man lynched in the 1800s. Next door to that building, the old deserted Maxey Hotel or Summy House, once a famous hotel, still held its old furniture including an old piano which locals said spooks would play during the dead of the night. Below: Skull on a stump in the window in Dexter.

During this time, especially because of the attention brought to it by the articles in the Dallas Morning News, Dexter became quite an attraction as a "professional" ghost town. People came from far and wide to see the attractions. This was its downfall according to town Mayor W. G. Delashaw. He was 76 years old in the early 70s and had lived in Dexter since childhood. He said after the newspaper articles, people mostly from Dallas came and stole all the coffins as souvenirs, broke windows in the old stores and hotel and even stole the human skull out of the window. Not only that, but the old doctor's office was the scene for the community dominoes game held there by residents for decades. They said the ghost hunters/**thieves** had even stolen their dominoes and some of the furniture from their old "game room." All this looting caused Mr. Delashaw to take the old patent medicines which were still on the shelves of the old drug store out and bury them for fear someone would steal them also. He did not want someone to BECOME a ghost by ingesting those old drugs and then be poisoned by them. Mrs. Delashaw removed the old piano from the old Summy House (which was once run by her parents) to save it from the looters.

The ghost enthusiasts got a very bad name in Dexter since they were rude when asked not to trespass and enter the buildings without permission or take things not belonging to them. They would drive up and stare at the townspeople, have picnics on Main Street (a functioning road), and litter everywhere.

What a shame.

The people of Dexter much preferred the ghosts to the ghost hunters.

It Looks Like and Acts Like a Ghost, It Must Be a Ghost - Assert Watchers of Dallas' Nightly Turtle Creek Apparition
– and Bigfoot too. But Chupacabra is a No-Show.

They weren't sure what was going on in the Turtle Creek and Oak Lawn districts of Dallas. Were people seeing ghosts, mental hallucinations, reflections of electric lights, or rising gas? But there were numerous very credible witnesses of some sort of specter.

Dallas Morning News, Jul 21, 1929 - To see the ghost, it was necessary to go to Irving Avenue beside the campus of Dallas University, near the brow of the hill, and look at a point a little south of east. The specter could be seen after 8 p.m. and was visible far into the night. The dim figure of a shadowy form was visible. It appeared as a semi-opaque formation of a human figure, silhouetted as the ghostly specter moved about appearing to dance one moment and wave about like a harvester scything grain. Witnesses were unable to explain its appearance. Turtle Creek at that time ran through that district and trees and underbrush formed a considerable wooded tract there. Some thought the apparition was merely swamp gas arisen from the rotten vegetation in the creek. Several people traversed the entire wooded tract and surrounding area on investigative tours but found nothing to explain the strange gaseous appearing form and the odd lights seen at intervals there.

Many were still saying there wasn't really a specter at Oak Lawn, but witnesses were inviting people to come see and they would then be convinced.

Seeing is believing. Or not.

Big "Little Rollo" Goes Ape in Oak Cliff

Another more corporeal phantom was at the same time terrorizing the Oak Cliff neighborhood creating a sensation. He was dubbed "Little Rollo."

Why he was given the name 'Little' was puzzling because he was said to be a GIANT ape or monkey prowling about in the treetops in the Dallas suburb, Oak Cliff. However, baboons are not known to be habitual tree-dwellers. They are found mostly in the ground in savannahs. Baboons can climb trees though, but they don't spend much of their time there.

Dallas, July 10, 1929 - A large ape some called a baboon had been making regular appearances in Oak Cliff. The latest sighting was made by a group of wide-eyed boys who reported Rollo pounced down from the trees into the middle of their marbles game ring, effectively putting an end to playtime.

For months, according to reports – unvarying as to description – the baboon had skulked about the Trinity River bottoms. After each public visit, he presumably retired to wherever he was residing in the trees.

Officials of local zoos had been checked over and over, but no apes or monkeys had been reported missing. (Lubbock Morning Avalanche.)

No one in 1929 was thinking about bigfoot or sasquatch, except perhaps Native Americans, but no one back then was asking THEM. Had they consulted the Native people; they might not have been quite so perplexed.

Sasquatch, unlike baboons, love to hang out (pun intended) around trees and river bottoms.

Man or monkey? Apparition or ape? Bigfoot or bogus? Missing link or escaped pet? I reported, you decide.

The Ghost Was Late In Dallas

Below: Cook family **dogtrot** home, in 1905, built much earlier.

Southern Mercury. (Dallas, Tex.), January 26, 1905 – During the pioneer days, it was customary to build houses of two rooms, separated by a wide hall, covered by one roof.

These two rooms had doors that opened into the hall, and no door for entrance from the front of the house; but instead, there were always large windows. In the later days, as timber and milled lumber became more available and cheaper, many of these old houses were remodeled. Some even added second stories, closing up the halls and adding other rooms at the back. One of these old houses was remembered by people as a haunted house. It was known that in earlier days an occupant had interred a baby underneath the front window of the east room of the old dog trot cabin. The place was rented out by a prominent real estate firm, and it had for many months been a "Jonah" to them, as they could hardly find a tenant for it, and the ones they did secure only stayed until the first full moon, then they would move out, bag and baggage and there was no getting any member of that household in the place again, and almost impossible to get them to even speak of their experiences.

People who knew what happened told stories of rattling chains, bloody scenes, awful noises or dreadful cries. One old tenant of the house who had stayed during one particular full moon and had moved out the very next day sat on a wooden crate sometime later and told his story to a rapt audience: "Yes sir, boys, that kid (the ghostly baby) just got up and took in every room in the house, downstairs and above, and after it had roused everybody for a block around, sailed out through the roof, and I just caught a glimpse of it as it passed on up into the moon."

Two young fellows who were out for a night's entertainment, and were familiar with the stories of the old house, decided that as the moon had just reached its zenith, they would try to see if they could not only see the ghost for themselves but see if they could kill or capture it (a useless hope, surely. How do you kill or capture a ghost? Who you gonna call?).

They had to build up each other's courage quite a bit as the hour approached and they armed themselves with a shotgun to be certain they were safe. At 9 p.m. they entered the haunted house and headed for the location where the window outside the old east room was which is where the ghost was said to be buried and from which it began its evening flights. The boy with the largest gun took his station there and the other boy patrolled the west room where the ghost was said to make its final ascent up to the moon.

It was soon discovered there was a hole in the floor of the east room. The full moon had now risen. The ghost was expected to also rise about 12 or 1 o'clock. Much to the chagrin of the boys, the ghost was late. By 1:30 one of the boys was ready to go home and sleep, the evening was a bust. The other said, "Let's wait until 2:30." It seemed like a week later, but it was only two o'clock when one boy felt his hair stand on end and his coat tail in the back raised up so straight that his cap actually moved down over his eyes, for he had heard the ghost; a little faint, weak cry like that of a very young baby just waking from a nap, and he heard it coming directly from the little child's grave under the window just as the stories had said. He listened and heard another cry, this time just a little louder and longer, and coming this time from the hole in the floor in the east room. The ghost catcher armed with his 10 gauge shotgun noticed with astonishment the hole was growing in size. The closer he brought the gun to bear, the larger the hole became, and his heart would pound just that much harder in tandem in a mighty effort to vacate his body. (In this case, the heart was wiser than the head!) After about a minute which seemed to stretch out for weeks, the cries finally centered themselves directly beneath the hole. After a moment of silence to let the tension build to a crescendo while the hunter tensely concentrated all his being on the evil hole, his heart seemed to cease beating altogether as the air was sucked from the room despite the open window. When the time was right, the cries began anew, echoing around the room, seeming to come from all directions, suddenly, shockingly, the hunter saw what appeared to be the head of a baby emerge from the cavernous crypt, wearing a hood, crying as if its heart were breaking, each cry more piteous and horrifying than the last. After the head had completely cleared the hole, the ghost hunter, at last, had a clear shot and pulled both triggers on his shotgun at once at close range. On hearing the shots, the partner of this ghost hunter who was upstairs hurried down, half a dozen steps at a time to see what had happened. The downstairs half of the team was very relieved to see him arrive. "Did you get him, old man?" the partner asked. Before he could answer, the double-barreled shot of the 10 gauge in the middle of the night in the haunted house had roused the whole neighborhood. Every male within earshot was arriving, demanding also to know what was transpiring. After explanations were made, all those present finally began searching for the remains of the ghost (assuming a ghost can be killed by a shotgun and the ghost has remains). They found just under the now-infamous hole, which had grown while the ghost hunter watched, had now inexplicably grown a further foot larger in every direction AFTER the shots. Inside the hole was found a long tail, four feet, a pair of ears, and numerous little pieces of yellow fur. No head was found, but after partial assembly of the remaining parts, it was postulated to be the remains of the largest yellow tomcat anyone had seen. No ghost baby was found, presumably, it escaped again up through the roof to the moon amid all the excitement, **using its "familiar," the cat, as a decoy. Outwitted by a ghost baby and a cat, how embarrassing!** Now the house will be inhabited by two ghosts, the baby and the ghost cat. Some MONTHS later, he was still being razed by people concerning the hunt-gone-wrong. The "ghost shooter" was heard to remark: "Not by a jug full. I've killed my last ghost. If you fellows want to make a hunt, you may do so alone, for I'm too fond of sleep to be caught in any such watch parties again." **He was probably tired of being the object of ridicule – outwitted and made a fool of by Tom Kitten and Baby Casper the Flying Ghost.**

East Dallas Haunted House

Fort Worth Daily Gazette, May 1, 1885 – New Caledonia, also known as East Dallas, had quite a big excitement over a haunted house. The former occupants moved out of it because of the tiresome habit of ghostly visitors slamming the doors at all times of the night. This made for very noisy, frustrating, wakeful, and frightening evenings. The tired tenants gladly vacated the premises hoping for a good night's sleep SOMEWHERE ELSE, ANYWHERE else! Hearing of this, (ghastly news travels fast), scores of people soon visited the place and concurred there was nocturnal strangeness in progress in the house. The police, being a much more pragmatic species of individual, believed tramps and petty thieves around town were the culprits giving the house its noisy bad name, hoping to drive out legitimate tenants and have the place to themselves. The fact that no arrests were being made did not change their opinion. Perhaps it was the ghosts who wanted the place to themselves, if so, they got their wish!

Now Fort Worth Must Respond In Kind With Its Own Haunting

The Standard (Clarksville, Tex.), & The Dallas Times May 15, 1885 –

Dallas has a haunted house. Now watch out for Fort Worth which will report three or four houses of the same kind, not to be outdone.

Dallas' Much Anticipated Ghost a No-Show

The Dallas Herald, March 10, 1887 - Eminent Doctor Cochran and Major Greenwall slept in a haunted house located on Griffin Street to catch sight of the ghost others had seen there. They said they wanted their hair to stand on end and have the sensation of having ice slip down their spine. However, they didn't see the ghost and the wished-for sensations had to only be imagined. They should know ghosts never perform on demand!

Always Investigate, Don't Be Used as A Dummy

The Daily Fort Worth Democrat, February 12, 1878 – One of the stores in the old dingy, dilapidated frame row on Main Street, between First and Second, occupied and used by Mr. Wiggins and his young wife as an oyster saloon and restaurant, was reported to have been visited periodically at nights with strange and mysterious moanings and noises, which seemed to fill the room, from whence no one could tell. At first, the sounds and voice were very indistinct and so low as not to attract particular attention. Mr. and Mrs. Wiggins retired at the usual hour to their bedroom at the back of the saloon. About midnight Mrs. W. was awakened by someone calling. Not being able to see who it was who was disturbing her at that late hour, she roused her husband. A futile search was made through the room and the employees were questioned, some of whom had heard someone calling, but professed ignorance as to the author of the sounds and voices. The strange sepulchral voice was heard frequently during the balance of the night and worked upon the nerves of the "Wigginses," so as to cause much uneasiness and insomnia. With the dawning of the day, the sounds disappeared, but the thought of passing one more fearful night preyed on the mind of Mrs. Wiggins who informed the police the following night and requested they stay close at hand. About midnight, the sound of the same voice again circulated through the whole room, several policemen were present and as a newspaper reporter showed up the very first thing the mysterious voice said "come up here you d—m old printorial sinner." That was a dead give-away, and everyone "tumbled" including the policemen, who quietly and quickly retreated. While two of them went to the rear of the house, one kept watch in the front, and the reporter utterly regardless of consequences, and covering himself with a mantle of assumed bravery remained inside to await developments. Several moments elapsed before the voice was heard again. Faint murmurings were soon distinguished in the air and policeman Baker, who was present was addressed with, "Baker you cultivated excuse for a 'cop', come out here." Just at this moment, the back door was pushed violently open and policeman Peters as he pointed to the new cook remarked, "There is the 'smart aleck'." He had witnessed the cook's trick of ventriloquism through the rear window. He was wasting his talents on cooking and ginning up fake haunted houses. He should have been giving shows with a dummy instead of making dummies out of everyone else.

Fort Worth Now Has Haunted House

Fort Worth Daily Democrat, October 4, 1881 - In 1878, there was a fake haunted house between First and Second Streets (as described in the previous story). Now there is a house on East Third Street known to be haunted. Once a place is known to be haunted, it obtains a bad name. If it's a rental property, it's value as such decreases to zero. Who wants to rent a noisy, terrifying insomnia producing domicile in which to live and PAY for the privilege? The occupants of this house for several nights had been disturbed by wild weird sounds, unaccountable noises, and scary groaning, tappings, and mourning cries. So great a fright did this produce that several gentlemen who were passing by were summoned to give aid and scare off the ghosts. The residents vowed they would no longer remain in a house where such fearful things were occurring. The intrepid reporters intended to check out the haunted house (from the other side of the street). The only odd thing about a haunted house is that hobgoblins seem to avoid their nocturnal antics whenever newspaper men are visiting, so they heard and saw no ghosts. However, in other news, the Fort Worth newspaper was happy to announce that while Dallas had recently announced their own stone woman in residence, somewhere. But Fort Worth could now say it had a bonafide haunted house, though they hadn't witnessed it, they believed the accounts! (More on stone and petrified men and women later.) Oh, the competitiveness between cities in all respects!

Haunted House Dare Gets Boys Into Trouble

The Paris Texas News on March 02, 1954, reported that four boys spent the night in a Dallas haunted house because of a bet. I bet they regretted it.

While there, they grew bored, not encountering any ghosts, so they began to snoop around. They rummaged through old newspapers in the boarded-up residence where they found an envelope containing $2,500 in cash and securities in the form of World War I Liberty Bonds, which they decided to keep. They divided the booty four ways, each buying a car, and all took a vacation trip to Galveston. All the money was spent except three bonds.

However, instead of installing them on Easy Street, this unexpected windfall landed them in the confines of the jailhouse.

See, I was right, they regretted it, but not for the reason I thought.

Beautiful Ghost of White Rock Lake

The Lady of the Lake

DALLAS - The famous park north of White Rock Lake has been a well-known meeting place for young people at night. Drivers say sometimes rocks were thrown at their cars, and even many police officers don't like to be at the park in the dark. It's just THAT creepy. It also doesn't hurt that many murders have also happened close by. Oh, and there are the drownings - after all, it's a lake!

This is where the dripping wet "Lady of the Lake" asks for a ride to a home on Gaston Avenue, only to disappear from your car. The big question is, is she a "real" ghost or was she a marketing ploy that took on a "life" of her own?

The story of the Lady of the Lake seems to start in the 1930s. Anne Clark wrote about the Lady of the Lake in 1943 in the book "Backwoods to Border." According to this, a young couple parked on the shore of White Rock Lake turned their headlights on and saw a woman in white coming toward them. She was a young woman dressed in a sheer, wet, white dress and had this to say: "I'm sorry to intrude, but I must find a way home immediately. My boat overturned. The others are safe. But I must get home." She got into the rumble seat, (seats old-fashioned cars used to have in the back) saying that she did not wish to get anything wet. She gave them an address on Gaston Avenue. When they asked her for further directions, they turned around to find the seat empty and wet. The couple went to the address she gave them. A man met them at the door and told them: "This is a very strange thing. You are the third couple who has come to me with this story. Three weeks ago, while sailing on White Rock Lake, my daughter drowned."

Here is another very similar version: Dallas author Frank X. Tolbert wrote a 1953 book called Neiman-Marcus, Texas: The Story of the Proud Dallas Store in which he wrote about this story. He also wrote a column in the Dallas Morning News where he wrote often about this ghost. In this account, a beautiful blonde girl appears on the road near White Rock Lake. He wrote about Mr. and Mrs. Guy Malloy, directors of display for Neiman-Marcus, spotting her standing as if she had just walked up from the beach. Upon seeing the girl standing in their headlights Mrs. Malloy said: "That girl seems in trouble. She must have fallen in the lake. Her dress is wet. Yet you can tell that it is a very fine dress. She certainly got it at the Store." The Neiman-Marcus store. The girl asked them to take her to an address on Gaston Avenue. When the car started, Mrs. Malloy turned to discover the girl had vanished. The only trace of her was the damp spot on the back seat. Puzzled, the Malloys went to the address she provided them. A middle-aged man met them at the door. He informed them that his blonde daughter, who wore nothing but Neiman-Marcus clothes, drowned two years before when she fell off a pier at White Rock Lake.

A more modern writer, Rose-Mary Rumbley, wrote that her dad, Guy Malloy of Neiman-Marcus, actually created the ghost story to promote sales at the store and the tale took on a life of its own. There really was such a man at the store at this time, how true the story was is up for debate.

Others say the original story of the Lady of the Lake predates the Neiman-Marcus story and is the result of a young woman who committed suicide in the Lake. This is a much more plausible explanation for the longevity and tenacity of the legend. It is not simply based on an ad campaign. Many others have claimed to see this lost female looking for a ride near White Rock Lake.

On July 5, 1935, Mrs. Frank Doyle found a suicide note left by her sister, Louise Ford Davis, who lived at the Melrose Court Hotel. Mrs. Doyle alerted the police, who sent seven squad cars to White Rock Lake, but they were too late. The Daily Dallas Times Herald reported "Detective Bryan, who was driving along the Garland road, turned on to the lake road [East Lawther Drive] and shortly afterward saw Mrs. Davis' head bobbing in the water. It was estimated that she had been in the lake five minutes when he [Detective Bryan] dragged her to shore." Although artificial respiration was employed in an attempt to revive Mrs. Davis, it was in vain and police remarked that if they had been called only "two or three minutes sooner," they might have saved her. The woman's car was parked nearby, a reporter added, and a "sheet and a pair of white gloves were found on the car seat." However, there was no mention of what she was wearing and the contents of the suicide note were not revealed.

On November 24, 1942, another woman, 35-year-old Rose Stone of Mansfield, Texas, committed suicide by drowning herself in the lake. Her body, dressed in a sweater and skirt, was discovered in eight feet of water near the municipal boathouse by Johnnie Williams, who assisted the park superintendent and city firemen in the search. A note was pinned to her sweater asking that relatives in Fort Worth be notified of her death. Mrs. Stone's coat and hat were found on the shore. So is Louise Davis or Rose Stone the "Lady of the Lake?" Is the ghost a young girl who fell off a pier and drowned, who lived had lived with her parents on Gaston Avenue and liked nice clothes from Neiman-Marcus?

The Downtown Dallas Adolphus Hotel

Built in 1912, specters have been reported by guests since the 1930s. The 19th floor is rumored to be the most active area of the hotel. The Palm Garden Ballroom once housed guests until a reconstruction project to add more rooms closed off what remained of the ballroom from the public. It is said that big band music and the sounds of people talking, laughing, and clicking glasses together can be heard coming from the sealed-off area. A ghostly bride is also believed to wander the hallways. She is believed to be a woman who was left by her lover on her wedding day, the bride (rather than live without her love), hung herself in the Grand Ballroom. She is seen in a wedding gown.

SIX FLAGS OVER TEXAS - Ghostly Sheets in the Wind In Arlington

The area where the famous Six Flags Over Texas theme park is located has a remote history before it was built by a wealthy Texas oilman, Angus G. Wynne, Jr. in 1961. It was meant to be scary in a fun, entertaining way, not a frightening, ghostly, supernatural way. But as we know, things are not always as we want them to be.

Ghosts have been seen in many places in the park over the years like the Music Mill, the Palace, the Candy Store, and of course, the old Log Ride.

One ghost in the park is a girl named Annie, who spends her time at the Candy Store as we would expect a little girl to do. The girl supposedly died before age 10 by drowning in nearby Johnson's Creek.

Annie has appeared occasionally in visitors' pictures. She hangs out at an old farmhouse that was included in the park. She has been seen by Six Flags employees turning the lights on and off in her "room," located in the yellow house near the entrance to the Texas Giant. Some have also seen her in Runaway Mountain.

Other classic "ghostly stuff" happens at the park, like inexplicable cold spots on summer days, being touched by phantoms; and doors, lights, and other ordinarily inanimate objects having a mind of their own.

BOO AT THE FORT WORTH ZOO

The zoo is believed to be haunted by former animal trainer Michael A. Bell who was crushed to death by one of the bull elephants at the zoo in 1987. Since this horrible accident, visitors to the zoo have reported seeing the ghost of a man walking near the elephant and zebra exhibits. However, Bell is not the only spirit haunting the zoo. There are reports of a lady in white 19th-century clothing with a parasol walking back and forth in front of the zoo café. It's hard to figure out why she is there since her clothing places her in the 1800s, so many years before the building of the Fort Worth Zoo (1909). However, there is a Frontier Village complete with historic vintage cabins at the entrance to the zoo, so it may have to do with those.

RIVER LEGACY PARK IN ARLINGTON, TEXAS

River Legacy Park boasts a couple of haunted places in the park. One is the **Screaming Bridge** in River Legacy Park. The history here is that a carload of kids was killed in a car accident with another car while crossing over the Trinity River on a narrow bridge. Both cars caught on fire and fell into the river, killing everyone involved. The road and bridge have been closed and can now only be accessed by walking through the park. People who are brave enough to walk over the bridge at night have witnessed tombstones in the water for each person killed, complete with their names at times. Other times, only lights are seen from the bridge, as well as a strange fog and creepy feelings. **'Hell's Gate'** is also in the River Legacy Park. This is a long trail that has swamps and large trees on either side. Legend claims that this was the trail walked by captured Union Army spies when they were being taken to be hanged. A red-haired apparition dressed in a Confederate General's uniform is often seen on a narrow path and people hear moaning off to the side of the track.

'Ghost of McDow Hole' in Stephenville, Erath County – 170 Years and Counting

The subject for this story originates in a place called McDow Hole or the Waterhole on Green Creek near Stephenville in west-central Erath County. The creek here is about twenty miles long and joins the Bosque River south of Stephenville, which is the county seat.

This ghost story has been told by many people in the old days, way back into the 1800s when Texas was a new state. You can find this story repeated in many modern publications as well since the life and the popularity of this story has stood the test of time. This writer was able to find an old article from Stephenville Empire-Tribune in September 1951 which laid out this story in a fairly complete way and referred to a book by someone who knew all about it. Joe Fitzgerald did a great deal to perpetuate the history of this ghost story and his daughter Mary Joe Fitzgerald Clendenin "wrote the book" about the Ghost of McDow Hole.

When the area around Green Creek was first being settled by white people, Jim McDow and his family moved near this waterhole perhaps in the 1850s, now known as McDow's Hole. Jim McDow died sometime before 1860, and one of Jim's sons in 1859 (according to a newspaper article) became lost in the woods, was found in a weak condition and died the next day.

Before Jim McDow's death, he had convinced his nephew Charlie Papworth, his beautiful wife Jenny and their infant son Temple to move to his land in Texas. Charlie had always wanted to move to Texas, but the malaria outbreak in Georgia and his Uncle's urging convinced him. Charlie found a spot on the banks of Green's creek opposite his Uncle Jim McDow's land who died shortly before his arrival in May 1860. Jim McDow Jr. was still there however to help them. The Papworth land went right down to the water's edge, and near the home, on the bed of the creek, grew a large pecan tree. This pecan tree would play a major part in the future of Charlie Papworth.

Charlie and Jenny soon had another child and in 1865. Shortly after the birth of the second child, Charlie received letters saying his parents had died and he was left their furniture. The only way to receive the furniture would be by train; but, at that time, Texarkana was the end of the line. Charlie had the things shipped that far but would have to go by wagon 200 miles to pick them up. Charlie went alone and Jenny stayed in the cabin by day caring for the two children and staying with the McDow's or their neighbors the Keiths at night.

When Jenny didn't go to either house one night, both families went to her cabin to check on her. They found Jenny and the baby missing and five year old Temple hiding under the bed in fear, unable to give a clear account of what had happened except the man responsible was white and spoke English. A search was made with no results.

Immediately, locals suspected a local ne'r-do-well, Civil War dodger, and coward named W. D. Brownlow who lived on the Bosque River as being the culprit. Some of his belongings were found near the Papworth cabin. He of course blamed the Comanches, but there was no evidence of that.

On his return, Charlie found his wife and baby missing and presumed dead with his son blaming a white man, and believed Brownlow responsible for their deaths. Brownlow knew the heat was on him, so he began to spread rumors about Charlie Papworth, saying he was a cattle and horse thief and perhaps even was the cause of this wife and child's disappearance.

Before too long, hooded vigilantes took Charlie and six other men in the middle of the night to lynch them. Some wanted to kill Temple Papworth too, but most would not have it. Temple, the boy, said he recognized the voice of the leader of the mob to be Brownlow. One by one, they hung the six men, and then lastly, they hung Charlie on the old pecan tree in front of Charlie's cabin and hurried away as daylight approached. Temple climbed up the familiar tree and cut his father down before he suffocated. Charlie and Temple borrowed a horse from their neighbor Mr. Keith to escape to Indian Territory.

Brownlow, ever after afraid Papworth would return and kill him in revenge, constantly committed petty thefts so he could be locked up in jail where he would be "safe" from retribution, but was forever haunted by fear.

Very soon after the Papworth's disappearance until the present day, strange things were said to happen around McDow's Waterhole. Mr. Keith had to regularly go to this watering hole for his water near the abandoned Papworth cabin. There were times when Mr. Keith and his son would stay at the cabin before heading home. One incident in the 1870s saw Mr. Keith and his 13-year-old son staying a few days at the abandoned Papworth cabin to save time while their cattle grazed and drank.

Mr. Keith, while sleeping in the Papworth cabin, woke up to scratching at the front door and he felt someone was in the house with them, but he could find no one. He also experienced a cold chill in the cabin and found that very strange since it was August. The next night he again awoke to the sound of scratching at the front door, he got up to open the door and there stood Jenny Papworth with her baby in her arms. He called out her name, "Jenny, is that you?" thinking she was alive and had returned. She then began to scream in horror and disappeared in thin air. Mr. Keith and his son were terrified and immediately left through a rear window, never to return.

Many credible witnesses, and some not so credible (or sober), say the ghost at McDow's Waterhole appears as a beautiful young lady, and some say she is a horrifying sight. A few years after the Keiths abandoned the cabin in fright, a coffin maker, of all people, decided to take up residence there. He knew about the ghost stories, but being in the "death business" himself, he wasn't afraid of such things. One day in the summer, some men were looking for their cows and went to ask the coffin maker if he had seen them there at his place, but no one answered the door. They checked on him, and lying in the middle of the floor, eyes wide open as if he had been staring up at something in horror, lay Charlie Atchison, dead. The doctor said he died of a sudden heart attack, perhaps from fright – scared to death by SOMETHING. Jenny perhaps?

Even tough train robbers are afraid of Jenny. In the 1880s the train had come to McDow's Hole. In the local saloon at Alexander, the nearest town, there was talk of the ghost, and Ruben and James Burrows, known for their reputation as train robbers worthy of Jesse James' repute, bragged they were not afraid of any ghost, especially a female ghost! They bragged they would go stay in the old Papworth cabin, no problem and bet money on it!

There WAS a problem.

I guess Jenny didn't like being mocked and minimized by these outlaws.

Once in the cabin, they saw Jenny walk right through the wall into the cabin then float up and out through the ceiling. It scared them so badly they said they unloaded their guns into the ghost (with no effect of course, why do people always try to shoot at ghosts?) then they ran from the cabin in horror and fear. They didn't go back to the town of Alexander out of fear of being the laughingstock of the community. They gladly forfeited the money they had bet. Jenny had the last laugh at their expense.

The young woman and her baby are sometimes seen at railroad crossings over the creek near McDow's Hole. Train engineers have said the woman and baby look so realistic when they appear, they have made emergency stops of their trains to avoid hitting them, only to realize there was no one really there. When they stop and investigate the area, no one is in the vicinity and there are no bodies on or around the tracks, she just disappeared.

In one incident in the 1880s, Engineer Sam Crow, and Fireman John Henson were on the Texas Central Railroad heading through this area. The Engineer made an emergency stop on the train tracks late in the night. The crew and passengers were upset and naturally wanted to know why. The engineer was shaking and emotionally stated he had just run over a young woman and baby on the tracks. The tracks and the entire area were searched with nothing or no one found. The underside of the train was searched for remains and none were found.

The baggage handler on the train reported he saw a blue apparition, through an open door in the baggage car, floating near the crossing at McDow's Hole and heard a woman scream during the same incident. The following night, the same woman and baby were again seen on the tracks and many more times since then at McDow's Hole. A young man in the 1890s who was working for Mr. Keith passed the waterhole one night on horseback on his way back from a dance in Stephenville. His attention was attracted by a pale green light moving along the water and the ground toward him. As it drew closer, it took shape – a beautiful young woman! As if this wasn't enough, she amazed the watcher by mounting his horse with him! His horse was understandably frightened by its ghostly rider and ran away wildly back toward Stephenville, (the young man was still on the horse too). When they all arrived back in town, the man looked behind him and the woman was gone! At this further shock, the young man fell off into the street in a dead faint and had to be revived by a bucket of water being dumped on his head.

This woman was seen by other passersby of McDow's Hole vaulting on to the back of a galloping phantom horse behind a ghostly rider who just happened to also be passing at the time. Sometimes she merely appears as a sad, weeping young woman holding a baby in her arms.

Mr. Brownlow, the man suspected of the murder of Jenny Papworth, died in 1885. He had moved to Dublin, Texas. In those days, people would sit with the dying.

Two people, including the local minister, were in the room while Brownlow lay on his deathbed. They said Brownlow would stare in horror and scream, "that woman! that woman! keep her away from me!" Then they saw the apparition of Jenny Papworth holding her baby at the foot of Brownlow's bed, tormenting him one final time, perhaps urging him to set the record straight. Shortly before he died, Brownlow admitted to killing Jenny and the baby because she had witnessed him conspiring with some known cattle rustlers, the very thing he had tried to accuse her husband of doing, even though Charlie Papworth was innocent. He said he strangled the mother and child then threw the bodies down a well near the creek. He covered the bodies with rocks so no one would find them.

But someone DID find them.

By the 1930s, the creek had changed course and a boy named Wes Miller made a discovery there – a hole that looked like an old well. Inside this was found glass buttons from a child's sweater and from a woman's dress. He also found a ring made from a dime that was supposed to have been worn by the Papworth baby.

A deep hole and heavy rocks couldn't hold Jenny and her baby down, could they? They didn't keep Jenny from haunting Brownlow for the rest of his life and keeping her story alive for all these years. Brownlow is long dead and turned to dust, Jenny is still being seen and discussed.

More Stephenville Strangeness

The haunting at the McDow Hole isn't the only strangeness around Stephenville in the little burg of Alexander. On June 1883, the Stephenville Empire reported J.F. Collier and three friends saw something amazing three miles north of Alexander: a coachwhip snake nursing from a cow. "All four men declared that they were ready to swear to what they saw."

The newspaper also believed they had found a missing child, though not alive, sadly. The body of a two-year-old Erath County boy who had vanished the previous fall had been found - in England - in a bale of cotton. It could happen! Especially to curious children. The newspaper noted the toddler had last been seen playing near a cotton gin before he went missing. People could fall into the machinery, be baled into a huge bale of cotton, and then be shipped on a boat halfway around the world. It's a terrible way to go! It's a high price to pay for free travel. They must have traced the cotton bale back to its source once they found the unfortunate stowaway.

Meteor - In May 1909, the Stephenville newspaper reported a meteor flying across the western sky. It lit up the town "with a brilliancy which would have enabled one to discern a pin in the street with ease." The newspaper also reported those who saw the meteor had been temporarily blinded. That's more than a meteor!

Plagues - Later that same year in August 1909 it had been raining grasshoppers near Cisco in Eastland County. "Showers of grasshoppers," the Stephenville newspaper said, fell like hailstones. Farmers built bonfires to burn the insects that appeared during the near Biblical plague.

Homicidal Elephant - When the Campbell Brothers Circus came to Stephenville in 1911, the newspaper said "an elephant stabbed a camel and killed him almost instantly. It is presumed he was tired and ill from several days' journey." We are presuming the elephant used its tusks and wasn't part of the knife-throwing act. As to the second sentence of the newspaper article, sounds like the elephant was in a VERY bad mood and wasn't taking any more attitude from that spitting foul-mouthed camel! Elephants never forget you know.

Ghost Dog in Stephenville! In March 1912, while walking down a Stephenville street at night, H.C. Barron stooped down to pet a white dog. But when he reached to pat the top of its head, his hand kept going as if the dog were not there. Then he realized, the dog was not there in physical form even though he could see it, it must be a ghost!

Ned the Little Green Man in the Cemetery at Aurora, Texas

- This settlement was about 27 miles north of downtown Fort Worth and began in the late 1850s. The beauty of this place impressed a man named William Stanfield enough to name it after the Roman Goddess of Dawn - Aurora.

The town became a trading center for the first twenty years of its existence and a post office was granted in 1873. Within 10 years Aurora had two schools, two hotels, two gins, and a population that may have reached 3,000. A spotted fever epidemic in late 1888 practically evacuated the town by 1889 and filled the cemetery with hundreds of meningitis victims. Then the Fort Worth and Denver City Railroad which was due to arrive in 1891 chose nearby Rhome for their depot instead of Aurora. This was usually a death-blow to a town as if the epidemic wasn't enough. Then came the alien in 1897. In about 1901, postal service was rerouted and the Aurora post office closed. There may have been nothing left of the town if not for the 1939 construction of State Highway 114.

In 1897, a local cotton buyer wrote a story about a crashed airship near Aurora and the recovery of "a little green man" (who didn't survive the crash) and was buried in the Aurora cemetery. The "airship" came crashing down into Judge Proctor's windmill on April 17, 1897, and burst into flames. Among the wreckage, Aurora residents found the mangled remains of what we would today call an alien creature. They decided to give him a Christian burial in their cemetery.

"Airship" sightings happened surprisingly often in the late 1800s. An account in the Dallas Morning News on October 5, 1898, reported that a 12-year-old boy saw "a great ball of fire" hovering about three feet over the ground with a buzzing sound before it took off again." In 1889, as Dr. J.M. Stephen's was going to Emerson from Paris, Texas, he saw an object that he said looked like a large balloon, about 100 feet in length, reported the Dallas Morning News. From the Dallas newspaper came another report in 1889: "Last night (at Grandview) about 11 p.m., a party fishing on Chambers Creek perceived the elements and the earth round about them as bright and luminous as noonday splendor...when three extra-large meteors were traversing the heavens in a northern direction. Just as they vanished and the iridescent beauty with them, three heavy sounds...nosier than the noisiest anvil firing were distinctly heard..."

What is the common denominator? Sightings only. No close encounters of the third kind.

Then came the Aurora sighting and crash. It was a close encounter of the third kind for sure.

There was a body!!

<u>THE GREAT AERIAL WANDERER</u> - A newspaper article in the April 19th Dallas Morning News included this information: "About 6 o'clock this morning the early

risers of Aurora were astonished at the sudden appearance of the airship which has been sailing around the country. They felt this airship had been seen several times before for several days all over Texas before it crashed. At Denton, this Dallas article and the Galveston News reported that a "mysterious ship" was seen "cavorting" through the sky in North Texas. A mysterious airship passed over Bonham, Texas at 3:15 a.m. on the same day in April of 1897.

"It was traveling due north and much nearer the earth than before." (This confirms this object or one very like it had been seen multiple times in this area before!) "Evidently some of the machinery was out of order, for it was making a speed of only ten or twelve miles an hour, and gradually settled toward the earth. It sailed over the public square and when it reached the north part of town it collided with the tower of Judge Proctor's windmill and went into pieces with a terrific explosion, scattering debris over several acres of ground, wrecking the windmill and water tank and destroying the Judge's flower garden.

The pilot of the ship is supposed to have been the only one aboard and, while his remains were badly disfigured, enough of the original was picked up to show that he was not an inhabitant of this world."

What made this story at Aurora stand out and stand the test of time for all these years? Not many, or any other than this one that I know of, of the old accounts of the time, mentioned having recovered creatures from the flying airships. There was a dead body in the craft, which was clearly identifiable as something non-human, but evidently intelligent enough to pilot a craft far beyond the understanding of the science of the time.

The cemetery is still there. Ned's grave is there too although his marker is said to have been stolen, so no one is even 100 percent sure where the alien was buried. Some even postulate his body was moved and sealed into the bottom of the well underneath the windmill into which he crashed.

Ned's Grave marker at Aurora

GOATMAN'S BRIDGE, DENTON

Old Alton Bridge, Argyle, TX

Goatman's Bridge, or the Old Alton Bridge as some call it, has a long history of scary and mysterious occurrences, going back to the 1930s. Many believe a half-goat, half-man lives near the bridge and terrorizes people near it. It is believed to be the ghost of a local goat farmer, who was lynched on the bridge by the KKK. After the hanging, people claimed there have been disappearances when people visit the bridge at night caused by the Goatman. There are people who also believe a young woman haunts the bridge searching for her lost child. Old Alton Bridge in Denton County was once the main path of transportation between residents of Denton and Copper Canyon. In the late 1800s, a successful black goat farmer named Oscar Washburn moved to the area with his family. He was known by people in the area as the "Goatman" and he put up a sign on the bridge saying "this way to the Goatman's" so people would know where to go to buy the best goats. This sign may have brought him business, but it also brought unwanted attention to himself. Klansman noticed a black man doing well and didn't like it. They kidnapped Washburn and hung him over the side of the bridge which carried his Goatman sign in 1938. When they looked down at his body, it was gone! The Klansman went back to town and killed Washburn's whole family. It's no wonder ghosts wander this bridge where such horrible tragedy occurred.

Another Goat Man Legend In Ellis County

A local legend here says that you can see a little boy along the "Goat Man Trail" in Italy. Supposedly, a little boy accidentally let some animals out of their pens. He got scared and tried to run away from the goat that was chasing him. On the way back to his house, a train hit him. Now, you might see him wandering around at night.

Many Hauntings in Waxahachie in Ellis County

A great place in North Texas to go for concentrated ghost hunting would be Waxahachie in Ellis County. One story says that the ghost of a confederate soldier walks down **Becky Lane** in Waxahachie at night. Becky Lane is supposedly the site of the last Union hanging after the Civil War. There are other places for ghost watching suited for staying a while and enjoying yourself in the process.

The old Ellis County jail (now relegated in the basement of the new facility) at 200 N. Rogers Street is said to be full to the brim with ghostly entities and stories. For a jail whose history goes back to the 1850's of the wild west, there would be no shortage of opportunities for the spiritual fallout of shootouts, hangings, murder, and mayhem.

The Catfish Plantation is probably the most famous haunted place in Waxahachie. It started as a beautiful Victorian mansion house. In 1984 it was purchased and converted into a great restaurant that caters to not only your appetite but to the paranormal. Stories say there are at least four different ghosts. They are Elizabeth, Will,

Ms. Caroline Mooney, and one named Lola Roller. The ghosts, at one time in their lives, resided at the house except for Lola Roller, who was murdered nearby, in a fit of jealous rage by a veterinarian in 1929. Both Caroline and Will died of natural causes while Elizabeth was murdered on her wedding day. Paranormal experts have investigated this place and most of them believe there are at least three ghosts in the house.

Guests here in the past have written their experiences at the restaurant in the guestbook. When you go, it would be entertaining just to read these entries. Some people have seen things move on their table, been touched by ghostly presences while there, heard knockings in the walls, walked into abnormally cold spots, and sometimes seen full apparitions. The manifestations here usually tend toward strange occurrences like kitchen appliances floating through the air seemingly of their own accord. That's strange enough for me!

The old Rogers Hotel in Waxahachie

The Rogers House, or Rogers Hotel was first built by Emory Rogers as a log cabin at a small town crossroads. Once the cabin was built, the Rogers home acquired a reputation as the family welcomed all travelers, and even Indians were offered a bed and a meal. The home served as the site of social gatherings such as religious and town meetings as well as a primitive inn for the area.

Before the Civil War, in the mid 1850s, the Rogers had a two-story wooden building constructed with the main entrance facing Main Street and a hallway that opened on College Street. The Rogers then placed an ad in the Dallas Herald that announced a "large and commodious hotel is now open to the public."

In 1870, John S. Siddons purchased the Rogers Hotel. The name was changed to the Waxahachie Hotel in 1877. But, the hotel manager at that time, Dr. J.W. McGee, a dentist from Dallas, left town shortly after the name change, and the hotel was reopened as Siddons Hotel. Siddons operated the hotel until 1881 after the Waxahachie Real Estate and Building Association purchased it for $5,500. The association then hired an architect to draw plans for a new three-story hotel. Within months of the announcement, the Siddons Hotel burned down on May 9, 1882.

Construction began on a new brick hotel that would be named Rogers House. The Rogers House was destroyed by another fire on Nov. 12, 1911. Reports state the fire was hard to control due to strong winds and low temperatures that caused fire hoses to freeze. (I have noticed a lot of haunted buildings burn down.) The current four-story building was constructed for $120,000 and opened in 1913 and operated till 1964.

This hotel is said to have had more than 300 ghosts in the building, famous, infamous and otherwise. The most known spirits are a cowboy, a little girl who drowned in the hotel pool, and Emory Rogers's son. Famous spirits include Frank Sinatra and Bonnie and Clyde. The little girl walks the lobby, while the Rogers' son haunts the elevator and the cowboy makes appearances in room 409, which is said to be the room with the most ghostly activity.

Here too, guests wrote down their experiences in the hotel. These records were kept in a book in the lobby along with newspaper and magazine clippings about Hotel Haunted.

There were also informational tours led through the hotel.

The building was restored around 2000 and now houses studio apartments and businesses.

Current residents also report the typical ghostly disturbances. For this reason, some residents don't reside there long.

Usually, paranormal experts who have investigated the hotel say the same thing - it is a portal to another world.

Want to get away, FAR away?

Northeast Texas

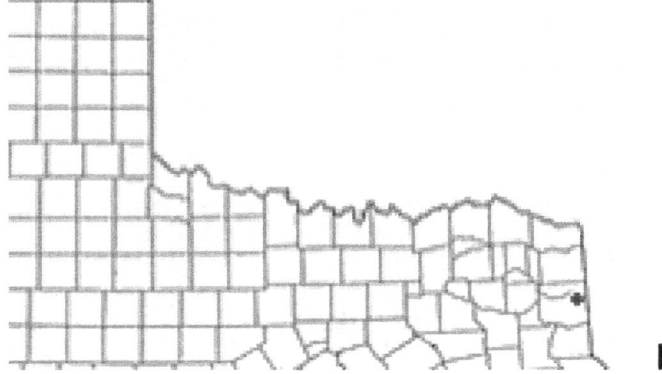

Karnack

Karnack of Texas

Texas has everything, even a little bit of Egypt, like the ancient city for which it is named. Karnack, Texas has another claim to fame – it is the site of former First Lady Lady Bird Johnson's family home, which is a national registered historic landmark.

This famous house also has another drawing card – it hosts a ghost.

In 1843, Milt Andrews built the plantation-style mansion two-and-a-half miles southwest of Karnak where he raised his daughter, Eunice, or "Oonie," as she was called. In 1880, when Oonie was 19, lightning struck the chimney, raced down the fireplace, burned, and killed her. This tragedy caused the Andrews family to sell the home to T.J. Taylor in 1902, the father of Lady Bird Johnson.

The ghost of Oonie Andrews was included with the sale of the house.

Oonie's ghost is still there in the bedroom where she died and makes creepy noises, moves objects, and makes unannounced appearances. Lady Bird Johnson was asked about Oonie's ghost and said, though she never saw the ghost, she felt a sense of apprehension and unease in the house as a child.

Karnack is not very far from Jefferson, Texas – a known hotbed of paranormal activity.

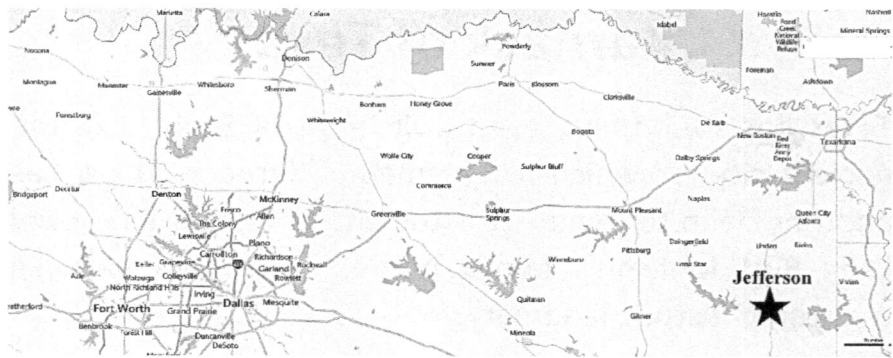

Jefferson's Ghosts

One of East Texas' most beautiful ghosts may be **Diamond Bessie**. Diamond Bessie, born about 1854 and murdered on January 21, 1877, was the popular name given to Bessie Moore, (Annie Stone). She was described as an extraordinary beauty with black hair and brilliant grey eyes who left home at age 15, taking up with a man named Moore. After they parted ways, she took on the life of a prostitute.

She eventually met Abraham Rothschild, who was of course very handsome. He worked as a traveling salesman for his father's jewelry business. His addiction to fast living and fast women soon included alcoholism, and his frequenting of saloons and brothels and all the trouble these bring with them. He became an embarrassment and a burden to his family. He met Bessie Moore in a Hot Springs brothel in 1875. From this time until her death, they were together. Theirs was an abusive relationship and ended badly. Rothschild was once arrested for beating her in public, and she accused him several times of trying to steal and sell her diamonds.

On January 17, 1877, the couple registered as husband and wife at the Capitol Hotel in Marshall, Texas, 18 or 20 miles south of Jefferson. After a few days, they traveled to Jefferson by train. Jefferson was, at this time, one of the largest and busiest river ports west of the Mississippi. They registered at the Brooks House in Jefferson as "A. Munroe and wife." Their fine clothes and Bessie's diamonds made an impression on the people of Jefferson of wealth and respectability so people would offer them credit and gamble with him. Rothschild is said to have first addressed his "wife" as Bessie during this trip, and this was adapted into "Diamond Bessie." The last person to see them together on January 21 was Frank Malloy, who noticed them in Henrique's Restaurant before 11:00 am. Malloy especially noticed Bessie's massive diamond rings. About three hours later, Rothschild was seen crossing the bridge back into Jefferson alone. The next morning, Abe ate breakfast alone at the hotel, where he was seen wearing Bessie's rings. On the morning of Tuesday, January 23, he boarded a train alone to Cincinnati, Ohio with his and Bessie's luggage.

Bessie's body was discovered in the woods along the Marshall road on the afternoon of February 5 by Sarah King, an African American woman out gathering firewood. She had been killed by a single gunshot wound to the head. The picnic lunch was still strewn about on the ground and her jewelry was gone.

Everyone suspected her 'husband' had killed her for the diamonds, though his conviction was finally overturned after two trials.

Diamond Bessie's grave in Jefferson's Oakwood Cemetery is a popular tourism spot. It stayed unmarked for years, but finally it received a tombstone, installed in the 1930s by a retired foundry worker, E. B. McDonald: "I placed it there one night because it did not seem right for Diamond Bessie to sleep in an unmarked grave."

A Diamond Bessie Murder Trial play is held in Jefferson to keep her story alive, but perhaps it is not just her story that remains to this day.

For years, there have been reports of Diamond Bessie's ghost around the Excelsior House in the Diamond Bessie Suite #104, but it hasn't hurt business at the hotel - quite the contrary.

Many believe Diamond Bessie herself stayed at the **Excelsior House Hotel in Jefferson**. But she is not the only ghost said to haunt this historic hotel, in fact, one of the oldest hotels in Texas.

There are the stock stories you usually hear about haunted places like smelling phantom scents in the air, people being disturbed in their beds, doors slamming, seeing lights and apparitions in the halls like women in black holding children, headless people, objects being moved on their own, etc.

There are many spooky rooms in the hotel, but the most haunted room is believed to be the **Jay Gould Room** because of a rocking chair which rocks on its own, and the door will slam shut on its own.

It has to be mentioned that Steven Spielberg was in Jefferson during the 1970s, filming his movie Sugarland Express. According to whispers and rumors on the internet, Spielberg stayed in the Jay Gould room where he threw his briefcase on a chair, only to have it thrown back at him, seemingly on its own. One morning, a little boy woke Spielberg up, asking if he was ready for breakfast. Knowing the boy was not "really there," Spielberg woke his crew up and left immediately. Is it a coincidence he did the film Poltergeist after his visit to the Excelsior House Hotel?

In an article in the Dallas Morning News on March 05, 1972, the cleaning lady for the Jay Gould room at that time, Ruby Britton, told the writer, Mr. Tolbert, that she would never enter the room alone, and then only in the day time. She always sensed a presence there with her, especially during rainstorms. She had once seen a headless apparition in the room. Personally, if I had seen that, I would never enter the room again, accompanied by another person or not! Ruby Britton wouldn't go into the President's suite alone either. Perhaps it was time for her to update her resume?

Tolbert consulted a ghost investigator in Dallas about the spirits in Jefferson. He said he had experienced many ghosts in the older northern wing of the hotel, like an unseen, heavy-breathing ghost who kept him up all night.

He visited another of Jefferson's old mansions and experienced many ghosts, some not so benign, especially at the ruins of the **old Haywood House near Big Cypress Bayou** and was the leading hotel in the days when the steamboats came up from the Red River and Mississippi. Jefferson was the second leading port then. Soon after the death of the owner of the Haywood House, $30,000 in cash was found hidden in the hotel. The same man had hidden money in houses and buildings all over Jefferson. The investigator went to the Haywood House right after the money was found and he sensed an evil presence and was in actual physical pain during the experience. He sensed many of the ghosts which had formerly been there were gone. (One man's opinion.)

Not Spooked by Spook House?

Dallas Morning News, Sep 30, 1951 – **In Frankston, Texas,** in between Athens and Mineola, Mrs. Lallie Carter, a stubborn redhead who didn't believe in spooks, moved into her "haunted" house and announced she was there to stay no matter what. (In an earlier story, we saw it didn't end well for people who mocked and scoffed at ghosts. They were often made to believe.)

Mrs. Carter prepared a proper "reception committee" for any ghostly, or other, characters who might be inclined to go around putting bloody handprints on the walls or marching noisily through the hallway. (Yes, you read that right, bloody handprints!)

Members of her welcoming committee, Mrs. Carter announced, included: a hearty skepticism, a double-barrel shotgun, a .38 caliber pistol, and a Boston screw tail bulldog named Midge. (Guns again, when will people LEARN??!)

Mrs. Carter inherited the house upon the death of her father. Her cousin J. W. Cely and his wife, were previously living in the house before Mrs. Carter took up residence. Mr. Cely said for three nights in a row, he and his wife heard phantom footsteps in the house.

Each time, their invisible guest left blood spots on the bathroom floor.

The third time, Cely armed himself with a shotgun and a flashlight and took up a hiding place in the darkened hallway. (Why do people always think they can kill a spirit with a gun? But in his defense, maybe he thought at first it was a regular mortal intruder.)

Mr. Cely said, "The footsteps kept coming toward me, and I waited until I knew I couldn't miss. I flashed on the lights. There wasn't anything there." (Oh, there was something there, all right!)

That time, he said, he found in the bathroom a perfect handprint on the wall – **IN BLOOD.**

Sheriff Roy Herrington said state laboratory technicians said the print was smeared in human blood and appeared to have been made by a woman with "long, slender fingers."

This was certainly no figment of imagination on the wall, it was real human blood!

The very next day, the Cely's moved OUT never to return!

Mrs. Carter said "I suspect it's just somebody trying to frighten me into selling the house cheap."

Easy for her to say when she didn't experience it herself. She would be lucky to sell it AT ALL!

I could find no article giving the results of her planned 'reception committee' for the ghost, but if I were betting on it, I would say that house soon went up for sale – **CHEAP.**

Buried Alive, Then Dead, In Frankston

At Dabb's Cemetery, near Frankston, there is a story of "the cage," where legends claim a man was buried twice, once alive and the second time dead.

Local people at the time claimed the man was buried the first time because he was thought to be dead, but dug his way out of his tomb and crawled to a nearby home, where he died.

What is scarier – getting buried alive and having to dig your way out, or burying a dead guy and having him crawl out of the grave to your doorstep, then opening your door to this dying dead guy?

To make sure he would not be able to crawl out again, a cage of wooden stakes was built around his grave. It worked as far as keeping his body under the ground, but there are still stories of a ghost roaming the graveyard late at night.

No cage can hold a spirit!

So if you see a dusty guy crawling around at the cemetery in Frankston next time you go by there, keep drivin'!

East of Athens is Frankston, southeast down the road from Frankston is Jacksonville....

A Ghostly Reminder of the Killough Massacre in Jacksonville, Texas

Fog in Texas, even in East Texas, usually doesn't rise and persist on warm, sunny days, except here in Jacksonville at the scene of a Massacre, now long past, but not forgotten. You know it's not a regular swampy mist when you see the Cherokee Indian on a horse ready for battle.

I came to know about this tragedy because the Killough family involved in this massacre is directly connected to cousins of mine from Denison, Texas.

This story begins in December 1837, a year after Sam Houston and his men defeated General Santa Anna at the battle of San Jacinto, which won Texas' independence. Issac Killough, Sr., originally of Irish descent, moved his family from Talladega, Alabama to East Texas and purchased land. The property had originally been part of a treaty settlement between the Texas Revolutionary Government and the Cherokee Indians negotiated by John Forbes, John Cameron, and Sam Houston. Many of the Cherokees didn't like the idea of giving their land away. Then in December 1837, the Senate of the Republic of Texas nullified the treaty.

East of Athens is Frankston, southeast down the road from Frankston is Jacksonville….

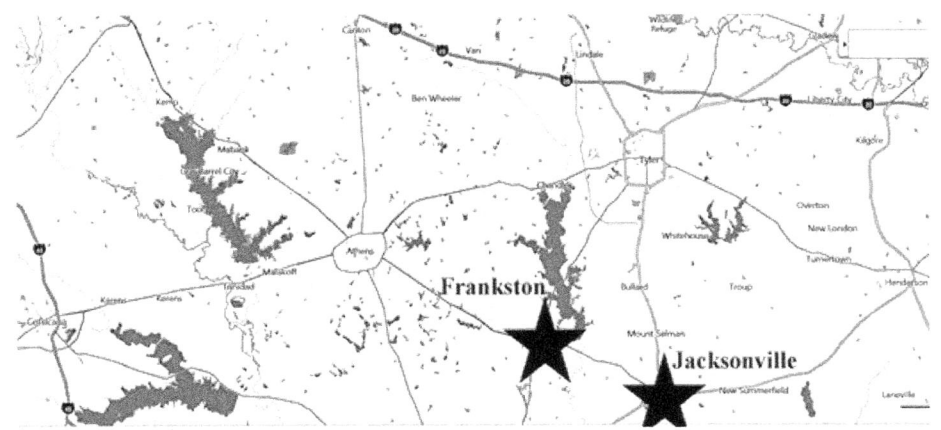

Conflict between the Texans and Cherokees was bound to happen at some point, and it didn't take long. On Christmas Eve, 1837, Isaac Killough was new in the area and might not have completely understood all this trouble with the Cherokees. His four sons, two daughters and their husbands, and two single men, Elbert and Barakias Williams all settled on the land. Very quickly, they built houses and planted crops on the land. Their corn was ready to harvest by August, but by that time, the Killoughs had heard from others they should protect themselves from attack by the Indians. It got so bad, the Killough family and other settlers had to move to Nacogdoches temporarily for safety. In about a month, they came back to harvest their crops. It was a mistake. They tried to agree with the Indians to leave them alone during harvest if they left by winter. Not all the Cherokees abided by the arrangement, because on the afternoon of October 5, 1838, near Larissa, north of Jacksonville, some of them attacked and killed or kidnapped eighteen members of the

Killough party, including Isaac Killough, Sr. I will spare you the gory details. The consequences of Indian attacks are not pretty. The survivors, which included Issacs's wife Urcey, fled to Lacy's Fort, forty miles south of the Killough homestead. When they arrived there, General Thomas J. Rusk organized a militia and went out in search of the Indians. Rusk's men caught up with them near **Frankston** where eleven of the Indians were killed. The Killough Massacre was the largest and most brutal Indian depredation in East Texas. The bodies that could be found were buried on the site. In the 1930s the W.P.A. placed a stone obelisk to mark the location. In 1965 the cemetery was dedicated as a Texas Historic Landmark.

People experience unaccountably sudden changes in temperature there. This is Texas, if it gets cold in July or August, you know something strange is afoot. Some people who visit this landmark in the daytime have uneasy, eerie feelings and want to get away from the area as if they are in danger. From what people say, you don't have to be a special investigator or intuitive to be affected by this place and sense something really out of the ordinary here. It's a creepy site, not to mention, the strange fog hovering over the area on a sunny day or the occasional visit of a phantom mounted Cherokee warrior. People who visit often suddenly have trouble with their phones. They say they can't call anyone, but their phones are making calls to people on their own, especially 911. (These calls to 911 come a little too late to save the Killoughs. Too bad the Killough family didn't have that opportunity in time to save themselves!). Paranormal investigators say they have detected strange electromagnetic anomalies around the site as well which may account for the phone malfunctions.

Killough Monument and Statue/Tombstone of Mother Templeton

The Weeping Tombstone at Jacksonville

If you go to Jacksonville to see the Killough Monument, don't miss a trip to the Old City Cemetery off Kickapoo Street. Ardelia Fuller, wife of J.A. Templeton, also known as Mother Templeton, was born in December 1853 and died in October 1910. Her grave is said to be haunted. People say sometimes when you watch her at night, her gravestone cries. She has a big statue as a headstone. Others say the statue changes positions in the moonlight. Sometimes the statue will be facing left, and at times right. Sometimes she will be holding a Bible, and at others, a bouquet of flowers. It's worth looking anyway.

STRANGE ANIMAL STORIES

Monster Bird Carries Child Away

This sounds like a pitch for a horror movie, but the truth is stranger than fiction, which is why I write non-fiction! This is scarier than a horror movie because it actually happened and…..could happen again! Horrors!!

What IS that up in the sky? It's a plane, no, it's Superman, no, it's a Monster Bird! RUUNNNNN! On December 8, 1890 the Fort Worth Gazette and December 14th, The Sunday Gazetteer in Denison Texas both reported this story: On December 5th, a monster bird carried a four-year-old child a distance of a mile before the bird was killed by the child's father in Italy, Ellis County. When news spread of the sighting of a bird large enough to lift a human being, the whole community was in a terrible uproar by the threat of this monster bird hovering over the town, circling round and round searching for a victim. It seemed no one was safe, especially children. Several men ran into the street with guns in a panic to help, but the bird was out of reach. Suddenly in one of its rounds, it was seen to descend with lightning speed into the yard of Charles Waller and grab his little four-year-old son in its talons and ascend slowly, but with seeming ease. The child's father, hearing the screams of the mother, ran to the house in time to see the monster carrying away his child. Grasping a gun, he mounted his horse in pursuit. The bird made direct for the Chambers Creek bottoms, about two miles distant, but after carrying the boy half the distance, its burden either became too great or too fidgety, and it slowly descended, lighting near a deep ravine. (Or perhaps it landed to kill its prey!) After the father took in the situation, he dismounted, crept up the ravine within a few feet of the monster, and shot it in the head. The child was relatively unhurt because the talons of the bird were fastened in the child's clothing, and when killed the bird was standing on the child's chest. The bird's body was **covered with a thin coat of hair**, with a tail, long-necked, like a crane, and weighed about 100 pounds. Was it really a bird, or was it a pterosaur?

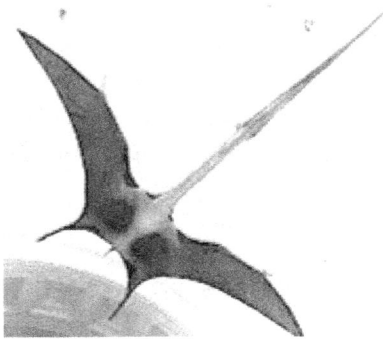

Think they were extinct in the 1800s? Maybe not, and maybe not yet. The Tombstone Epitaph in 1890 reported a creature matching the description of a very large pterosaur being seen and killed there. People have searched for the photo of the monster nailed to a cabin wall that was rumored to have been taken at the time. There have been several photos put forward as the original, but no one yet knows.

Below: a Civil War-era picture of soldiers standing over a dead Pteranodon. This photo is believed to be genuine and has been widely circulated. There is another similar (but inferior) picture on the internet, but it was from a movie/show depicting this original scene. Then a close-up of the head.

Huge Eagle Carries Off Child

Honey Grove Signal (Honey Grove, Tex.), Dec 18, 1925 - John McGrady, who lived north of Bonham, Texas near Red River, captured a golden eagle a few days previously. The eagle had earlier grabbed a child, taking him up in the air a few feet, but the child was rescued before it could be carried off. McGrady shot and crippled the eagle and then caught it. The eagle measured seven feet from the tip of its wings. The huge bird was taken to Bonham and auctioned off. The eagle had also been known to have carried away several pigs and lambs.

Huge Eagle Carries Off Child

Honey Grove Signal (Honey Grove, Tex.), Dec 18, 1925 - John McGrady, who lived north of Bonham, Texas near Red River, captured a golden eagle a few days previously. The eagle had earlier grabbed a child, taking him up in the air a few feet, but the child was rescued before it could be carried off. McGrady shot and crippled the eagle and then caught it. The eagle measured seven feet from the tip of its wings. The huge bird was taken to Bonham and auctioned off. The eagle had also been known to have carried away several pigs and lambs.

Eagle With 8-Foot Wingspan

The Meridian Tribune (Meridian, Tex.), January 3, 1947 - A Mexican eagle with an 8-foot wingspan was killed by Blanton Copeland on the Graham Cole ranch near Meridian Bosque County, Texas. Copeland said he shot the monster bird when it swooped low over him as if it were hunting him. It weighed 18 pounds, had talons around three inches long, and appeared to be large enough to take away a half-grown lamb. Good thing no children were outside that day.

TOUGH CHICKEN

How long can a chicken live without food or water? Ever wondered? Yeah……. me neither. But in case you are curious to know, this article may be of value or just some interest.

Honey Grove Signal (Honey Grove, Tex.), January 22, 1926 - During Christmas week Robert Shelton missed one of his hens and one of his roosters. Chickens have a way of straying off at times, and occasionally a poultry yard is invaded by prowlers (hungry predators), and so Mr. Shelton made no extensive search for Biddie and her husband (the rooster). They were not in their accustomed place, and he took the loss of two chickens as gracefully as possible. In the poultry-yard was a big washtub, and this tub had been left standing on the side to dry and sun. The rooster and hen, perhaps, were searching in the neighborhood for worms, when an unfriendly wind must have blown the tub down and covered and held prisoner the ill-fated chickens. Finally three weeks later, this last Thursday, Mr. Shelton had occasion to move the tub, and lo, when he turned it up, there was the long-lost hen and rooster. The rooster had long since ceased to live, but the hen was alive, though very poor and weak and also blind. She was induced to take a sip of water and a little food, but starvation had done its work, and she died the next day. This beats the previous area record of two weeks, but that story had a happier ending.

Several years previous to this, a tornado came through this area and reduced the home of Baxter Roddy, near town, to kindling wood. It blew a sitting hen across the road and covered her up with debris. Fourteen days later, when the debris was removed, the hen was alive and able to get about. She lived, and perhaps incubated and reared several happy families following her close call with death.

The Shaggy Dog

Whitesboro News, March 09, 1888 – This newspaper reported a ghost story they labeled as "very plausible." It was said a man named Williams, who had recently died near Winona in Smith County Texas had reappeared in the form of a shaggy dog. He would enter a room suddenly and mysteriously and when touched; he would vanish into thin air. Their assessment of Mr. Williams was that if there ever lived a man who would like to create a postmortem disturbance, Williams was that man. They were not surprised by the report.

Just Plain Weird, Strange and Creepy Stories

The Stuff of Nightmares - Buried Alive

The Bonham News. (Bonham, Tex.), April 26, 1901 – A horrifying accident occurred in Durant in the Choctaw Nation near the Red River which resulted in the tragic death of four boys. The mode of their deaths is the stuff of nightmares made into a reality.

James A. and Pressly Rhodes, aged 13 and 14 years, respectively; Claude Etheridge, aged 15; John Bain, aged 13 were killed as a result of the accident. Also involved in the accident was Claude Bain, aged 15, who turned out to be a heroic survivor of something seemingly impossible to survive.

For some time, these boys had been using a bluff bank on a little creek that flowed about half a mile east of the Missouri, Kansas and Texas depot, as a playground. They had made a large excavation in the bank and had divided it into rooms, making quite an extensive cavern, extending very far back into the bank. In the afternoon the boys were playing in the cave house, when the ground, made of sandy loam, softened and made weak by the recent heavy rains, began caving in, and in a short time the mouth of the cavern was filled and the dirt began falling in the rooms partitioned off in the cavern playhouse and before the boys realized what was happening, or had any sense of the extent of the danger they were in, the earth had completely covered them.

Claude Bain was one of the first to realize what had happened and that death was certain if he did not get out of his precarious predicament in short order and without losing his head, or being overcome by fright, he set to work to try to find his way out.

When one is in this situation, in total darkness and silence, it is easy to lose one's sense of direction. This is made worse when one considers they are only children and there is no air. Panic can take over.

Claud Bain was separated from his companions by the dirt that had fallen, filling the excavation, and luckily, when he started to work his way out, he chose the right direction.

The boy used his hands with almost superhuman strength, scratching sand and dirt from in front of him and pushing his body forward with all his might in the direction he thought to be right, and in a few minutes, he was rewarded by seeing the sunlight. As soon as he was on the outside, he saw that any efforts of his own to save his companions, would be fruitless and useless, and he started to Durant as fast as he could run, giving the alarm. In a short time, the news had spread about the town, and a large number of men went to the creek bank and began the work of removing the fallen dirt and trying to reach the imprisoned boys before it should be too late to render them any assistance. The earth was removed and the bodies discovered. They could see some of the boys had not been so stunned by the initial cave-in that they had not tried to get out, but they, unfortunately, were digging the wrong direction and were suffocated while they were digging. It was not an hour from the time the creek bank caved in till the bodies were taken out dead.

The creek bank where the boys were suffocated is about half a mile east of the M. K. & T. depot at Durant, and almost within the limits of the town. The earth which is firm in dry weather was saturated by the rain that had fallen for about twelve hours, and this caused the caving of the bank after the boys made their excavations, which had further served to undermine the bank.

The boy who survived must have spent a lifetime of terrible memories and worse nightmares, and he was the lucky one. The last moments of the deceased boys must have been horrible.

Death Test?

The Savoy Star. (Savoy, Tex.), April 23, 1915 – The fear of being buried alive was for many years previous, and still was at this time, so widespread that the French Academy of Science some years previously offered a cash prize of $7,500 for the discovery of some means by which even the inexperienced might at once determine whether, in a given case, death had ensued or not. A physician obtained the prize. He had observed the following well-known signs: If the hand of the suspected dead person is held towards a candle or other light, with the fingers extended and one touching the other, and one looks through the spaces between the fingers towards the light, there appears a scarlet red color where the fingers touch each other, due to the blood still circulating. It shows itself through the tissue which has not yet congested. When life is entirely extinct, the phenomenon of scarlet spaces between the fingers at once ceases.

Thank you for reading my book, I hope it has been interesting and informative for you. I hope you will want to read more about this wonderful area! I have many books about the history of the people and the area I love.
They include:
Coming soon: When the West Was Wild in Gordonville and Cedar Mills (Wild West Vol 6)
When the West Was Wild in Delaware Bend (Wild West Vol 5)
When the West Was Wild in Pottsboro Texas (Wild West Vol 4)
Gone With the Water ... The Saga of Preston Bend and Glen Eden
Crime & Calamity in Preston Bend When the West Was Wild Vol 3
When the West Was Wild in Denison Texas (Wild West series Vol2)
When the West Was Wild in Pottsboro Texas (Wild West Vol 1)
Quantrill's Raiders In North Texas & Jesse James Gang in Grayson County Texas
The Many Faces of Texoma's Red River
Pottsboro Texas and Lake Texoma, Then and Now Volume One and Two
School Days Around the Pottsboro Area & NW Grayson County

Ghost Towns of Texoma, Vol 1 – Preston Bend
Ghost Towns of Texoma, Vol 2 – Hagerman
Ghost Towns of Texoma, Vol 3 – Martin Springs
Ghost Towns of Texoma, Vol 4 – Georgetown, Fink Ghost Towns of Texoma, Vol 5 - Locust, Willow Springs
Reflections on the Beauty of Lake Texoma
Texoma Tales Volume 1 – NW Grayson County's People & their Stories
The Old Country Store
True Ghost Stories of Grayson County Texas...and Other Strange and Scary Tales Volumes 1, 2, 3, 4 & 5

I am, God willing, intending to write many more history-related books, since we have such a rich heritage here, and I am sure I will only scratch the surface. People ask me why I don't think I will run out of material. I respond, there have been a LOT of people in this area and they ALL have a story. I have given several local history related speeches and costumed living history presentations.

All my books are available on:
Amazon.com, my author name is Natalie Clountz Bauman,
On etsy.com from the store PottsboroTexasBooks
You can order books directly from the author
and you can get the books in Denison on Main Street at The Book Rack and The Main Street Antique Mall;
in Sherman at Touch of Class Antique Mall
They can also be found at the Frontier Village Museum at Loy Park in Denison and at my personal event appearances. I also have a tour company called Red River Tours. We give Ghost Tours and Wild West Tours. **To get tickets, go to our Facebook page Red River Tours.** Thank you for considering my books. I hope you find them interesting and informative. God bless you!

Made in the USA
Las Vegas, NV
07 April 2021